FAITH at WORK

Christian Vocation in the Professions

EDITED BY DAVID W. LOY

3558 S. Jefferson Ave., St. Louis, MO 63118-3968
1-800-325-3040 • cph.org

1 2 3 4 5 6 7 8 9 10 32 31 30 29 28 27 26 25 24

PRAISE FOR *FAITH at WORK*

What a wonderful way to express the vocation of a Christian university: by enlisting faculty to write about vocation in very meaningful and specific ways! David W. Loy has recruited a team of knowledgeable Lutheran faculty to explore the meaning of vocation in the rich Lutheran tradition and then express how Christians exercise their vocations in a wide variety of professions, from teachers to pharmacists. The various writers show not only how Christians become conduits of God's love in their places of responsibility but also how they bring to bear the Christian intellectual and moral tradition in those callings.

Robert Benne, Jordan-Trexler Professor of Religion emeritus, Roanoke College; professor of Christian ethics at the online Institute of Lutheran Theology

Faith at Work will help professionals, pastors, and professors reconsider the roots, motivations, and orientations of work and every vocation in light of the Christian narrative. What does the Bible reveal about work and vocations? How do vocations affect individuals and communities? Can economic systems stymie or assist vocations? What does professional education lack in a secular age? How can I lean in to my profession as a call from God for human flourishing? This book sheds lights on questions like these and on several specific professions, providing examples easily applicable to many others.

Scott Ashmon, PhD, MDiv, senior vice president and provost, Concordia University Irvine

CONTENTS

ACKNOWLEDGMENTS

This book was made possible in part by a generous grant from the Kern Family Foundation. The grant enabled the authors to meet in person to discuss initial drafts of our chapters, and it helped underwrite other costs associated with this project. I wish to thank the Kern Family Foundation on behalf of myself and the other authors.

Concordia University Irvine has been a particularly fertile environment for the development of this book. The seeds were planted a decade ago when Steve Mueller, Scott Ashmon, and I began talking about the "Vocation and Ethics" initiative. Faculty from across the university helped water and nourish the budding project with our ongoing conversations about the Lutheran intellectual tradition and the nature of Lutheran higher education. Members of the graduate-programs reading group nurtured the project to the point of fruition. Some of them contributed to the volume. All of them helped shape it. Steve, Scott, and members of the reading group, thank you for your encouragement, friendship, and wisdom.

Laura Lane at Concordia Publishing House has provided sage advice starting with my first inquiry, and she mediated between various teams at CPH and me to help develop a book that will be a blessing to three rather different audiences: current professionals, graduate students aspiring to become professionals, and pastors. Laura, thank you for our brainstorming sessions and for entertaining my unusual ideas for publication possibilities.

Jamie Moldenhauer, my editor at Concordia Publishing House, took on a project that involves not one but three-and-one-half different citation styles. Jamie, thank you for your attention to detail and your willingness to learn a little APA and Bluebook.

Finally, although this project has been years in the making, the final stages came at a particularly busy time for my wife and me. Mary, thank you for the sacrifices you made so that I could finish the manuscript during this busy and unsettled season in our lives.

INTRODUCTION

David W. Loy

What difference does God make to our work? And what difference does our work make to God? For Christians, who hope to live in a manner pleasing to God because Jesus redeemed us by His life, these two questions have particular significance. We hear God's Word in public worship, and we read God's Word during personal devotional time, and then we move into the mundane activities of everyday life, including our jobs. We know that God wants us to love others and act ethically in our jobs, but non-Christians can do the same thing. So what difference does God make to our work? And to Christians who work in "secular" jobs—that is, who do not work in church-related ministries—it may seem that their work is not all that important to God. Their work does not, in and of itself, show people the way to heaven or help people grow in faith in Jesus. So what difference does their work make to God?

This book is driven by two convictions. First, God makes a great deal of difference to our work. God created us, and He placed us into a world that has all the resources necessary for us to survive and flourish. Those resources come from His gracious hand. We have the privilege of gathering those resources, learning how to use them in new and creative ways, and building a flourishing world under God's continuous care. Most remarkably, He gives each of us talents and abilities useful for contributing to this grand project of caring for one another by building a flourishing world. What difference does God make to our work? He provides all we need to accomplish it, and He calls us to trust His gracious provision as we undertake our work as a means for caring for one another. Unfortunately, since the fall into sin, we fail to trust God as we ought, and we therefore turn against one another. We fail to seek the flourishing of all. God's response was to send His Son, Jesus, to bear the just penalty for our turning against Him and turning against one another. Jesus died at our hands and rose again from the dead on the third day to reconcile us to God the Father and to one another. The love God showed through His Son, Jesus, moves Christians to strive to trust our gracious God more fully and to show His care to all. We show that care in part by taking up the tasks placed before us in our jobs with a renewed vision for helping other people flourish under God's gracious provision.

The second conviction driving this book is that our work is important to God. The God who created the world out of nothing, the God who formed dust into a human shape and then gave it human life—this same God has chosen to provide for each human being through other human beings. Our work is the conduit through which God provides for our life in this world. Martin Luther put it this way: in our work, we are "masks of God" through whom He is at work to provide everything we need for life.[1] When I do my work poorly, then I detract from God's gracious provision for me and all other people. When I do my work well, God blesses my work in order to provide graciously for me and all people. And every human being is important to God, because He created each of us and sent Jesus to reconcile each of us to Himself. Thus, our work is important to God, because through it He lovingly provides for other human beings. This is true no matter how lowly or mundane our work may seem in the eyes of other people. Under God's gracious provision, house cleaners and custodians have jobs that matter every bit as much to God as preachers and presidents. All honorable work is clothed with dignity because God uses it to provide for the human beings He created and redeemed.

These two convictions are core components of the doctrine (or teaching) of vocation. This book is directed to professionals, students aspiring to be professionals, and pastors who preach to professionals. The goal of the book is to unpack the significance of vocation for the work of professionals. This task is particularly important because the education necessary for becoming a professional rarely, if ever, articulates the relationship between God's work in the world and the work of professionals, so Christian professionals often lack an understanding of the difference God makes for their work and the significance their work has to God. Professionals and aspiring professionals will find that

1 *Luther's Works* 14:114.

this book places the technical skills and ethical norms of their (desired) occupations into the broader context of the Christian faith, helping them to see how God is working through them to build a more flourishing world for all people. Pastors will find that the book offers them insight into the "thought world" of the professionals in their congregations as well as the challenges and joys professionals face, helping them preach and teach the good news of God's love in Christ more concretely.

The book is divided into two parts. The first part contains chapters that address the vocation of work and the work of professionals from theological and economic perspectives. Chapters in the second part address specific professions. Each chapter can be read on its own. However, the chapters address the lives of professionals from a variety of angles, and no chapter is so specific that practitioners from other professions cannot learn from it. Together the chapters create a mosaic that depicts the myriad ways in which the Christian faith informs the work and lives of professionals. As editor, I therefore encourage professionals and students and pastors alike to learn from the wisdom of all the faithful Lutheran-Christian theologians and professionals who have contributed to this volume by reading all the chapters.

Professionals and the Professions

Words and phrases like "profession," "professionals," and "the professions" invite confusion because they are used in conflicting ways in English. The word "profession" is sometimes used in place of "occupation," as in the question "What is your profession?" This use of the word can encompass nearly any occupation (although it has overtones of what we might call white-collar work). The word "professionals," on the other hand, when applied to specific jobs in the workforce, typically refers explicitly to white-collar jobs. Thus business people and doctors are called professionals, and the phrase "professional dress" clearly communicates the kind of clothing people in business would wear to a work meeting, not the kind of clothing tradespeople (plumbers, electricians, and other skilled workers) would wear in the course of their work.[2] We might call this use of the word "professional" the broad sense of the term.

The phrase "the professions" has been used in a narrower sense to describe occupations that meet several criteria: (1) They require a high level of education in a specific domain not easily accessible to those without said training. (2) Prior to practicing these occupations, an individual must be licensed by an appropriate body (typically, but not always, independent of the state) composed of people already practicing in the respective occupation. (3) Practitioners of these occupations are subject to a code of ethics developed by that same body (or another body also composed of people practicing in the profession) and are subject to discipline by the body if they violate the code of ethics. (4) Members of the public entrust practitioners of these occupations with sensitive information or direct access to their bodies because of their education and licensure. (5) Practitioners of these occupations have a fiduciary responsibility to use their knowledge and skill for the benefit of their clients while holding in strict confidence all information disclosed to them in the context of the relationship. (6) Practitioners have a strict duty not to misuse the power inherent in their relationship for their own benefit. The three traditional professions in the West are law, medicine, and theology. Today nurses, mental health therapists, financial advisors (CFPs), tax accountants, and marriage and family therapists are also members of the professions.

It is the distinction between the professions and professionals that leads us to judge more harshly when a doctor or pastor takes advantage of a patient or parishioner than when, for example, an accountant takes advantage of someone who reports to her. Both cases involve wrongdoing, but the accountant (who is a professional in the broad sense) has simply abused her power, whereas the doctor or pastor (who is a member of one of the professions) has not only abused his power but also violated the trust placed in him.

2 The word "professional" is also sometimes used to refer to athletes and artists who receive payment for their work. It can also refer to an individual who conducts his or her work with great skill acquired through extensive experience. This latter meaning is what I have in mind when I give up fixing the leak under my sink and say it is time to call in a professional—I am not referring to the plumber's occupation in this case but to the plumber's skill and experience.

This book is aimed at members of the professions as well as professionals in the broad sense. Members of the professions face certain unique challenges because of potential conflicts among their professional autonomy, personal convictions, and the desires of their clients; the chapters addressing these specific professions will explore those tensions. However, those in the professions and professionals in the broad sense face certain common challenges as well, especially in understanding how their specific work contributes to human flourishing. This book will therefore show the unique contribution that professionals (including members of the professions) make to building a flourishing world for all human beings.

Vocation

The word "vocation" also has a confusing variety of meanings in the English language. "Vocational training" generally refers to training for specific trades or skilled labor positions. "Vocation" is sometimes used as a synonym for "occupation." And members of certain professions sometimes claim that their profession is not just a job but a vocation. The Lutheran tradition offers a unique understanding of the word "vocation" that is grounded in Scripture and provides helpful guidance for professionals. "Vocation" (from the Latin *vocare*, "to call") refers to God's call to serve our neighbors as Christ has served us. Each individual receives that call within a specific set of social circumstances, as a participant in a unique set of relationships, and as the possessor of specific talents and abilities, so the call has a unique shape for each individual. In fact, Lutheran theologians contend that each set of relationships an individual has is a unique vocation. If you are married, "spouse" is one of your vocations. If your parents are still living, then "adult child" is one of your vocations. "Citizen" is another of your vocations. God calls you to serve the people in each of these vocations in ways appropriate to that vocation.

By this definition of "vocation," work (that is, paid employment) is one of many vocations an individual may have. That is, work is a social role in which God calls us to serve others as Christ has served us.[3] This definition suggests that work is important to God, whether that work involves telling people about Jesus or not. Work is important to God precisely because it serves those whom God created and whom He reconciled to Himself through Jesus Christ.

Different chapters in this volume take different stances about the relationship among feeling called to an occupation, having a sense of passion for an occupation, and the occupation as a vocation. Some of the authors emphasize the objectivity of our vocations. That is, they emphasize the fact that our vocations typically confront us as facts in our lives about which we simply have no choice. No child chooses his or her parents, for example, nor does a child choose his or her siblings (or, in fact, whether he or she has siblings). Even vocations we typically choose come with unpleasant tasks we are to fulfill out of love for the individual served in that vocation. For example, my passion, or lack thereof, for changing my infant children's diapers was quite irrelevant to whether I was called to change their diapers—and I most certainly was called to change their diapers, both as an act of love toward them and as a mask of God through which He cared for them.[4]

Yet the fact is that many individuals in our society enjoy the opportunity to choose an occupation. Individuals choose on the basis of any number of criteria, including likely income, expected sense of satisfaction, anticipated experience of helping others, and hoped-for chance to engage in activity one finds immensely enjoyable. The sense that I may be particularly suited to one occupation rather than another because of my talents and abilities, or the feeling that I would derive immensely more satisfaction from one occupation than another, can be experienced as a sense of calling. However, this subjective sense of calling is not enough to require others to hire me into my preferred occupation—and, in fact, my sense of calling can turn out to be wrong.[5] And it is not

3 Work that violates the norms of God's Word, such as producing or distributing pornography, cannot be a vocation by the definition used here, because God will not call someone to violate the norms of His Word.

4 For an eloquent encomium upon the call from God to change diapers, see Martin Luther's treatise "The Estate of Marriage" in *Luther's Works* 45:39–41.

5 See Curt Gielow's essay "A Vocation of Service: Healthcare Administration" in this volume for an

until I am actually *in* a job that the job becomes another of my callings from God, another of my vocations. That is why every author who contributed to this volume would agree that the *sense* or *feeling* of being called to an occupation is not a constitutive component of vocation.

The golden thread that runs through all the essays in this book is this: vocation is the call from God to serve those entrusted to our care in the roles in which we find ourselves. In these vocations, we are masks of God through whom He shows His love by providing what we human beings need for life in this world. Christians understand that our service in our vocations flows out of the love God has shown us in Christ. Vocation is ultimately defined by the God who calls us, sometimes through our desires and choices, and sometimes apart from them. "Our gifts do not always turn out to be what we want, what our souls are craving. But the gifts we receive often enable us to better serve our brothers and sisters in Christ. Equally so, our gifts are a reminder of the ultimate gift we have in Christ—His saving death and resurrection—a gift that we receive, not through deeds but through grace and faith."[6]

---

account of just such a mistaken sense.

6 Emma Johnson, "Grace Alone" (devotion, Concordia Irvine, October 17, 2023).

PART 1

VOCATION *and* HUMAN FLOURISHING

THE WORKING GOD IN THE OLD TESTAMENT

Paul M. C. Elliott

Rev. Paul M. C. Elliott, PhD, is Associate Professor of Theology at Concordia University Irvine. His teaching, research, and publications are focused on the Old Testament. He was assistant pastor of St. John Lutheran Church in Aurora, IN, before coming to Concordia.

> Unless the LORD builds the house, those who build it labor in vain. Unless the LORD watches over the city, the watchman stays awake in vain.
>
> *Psalm 127:1*

The Old Testament may seem like an odd place to seek vocational advice. Ancient Israel was a premodern, agrarian society with very limited career choices or social mobility. They had nothing like a modern market economy. Most of the professions of the twenty-first century were not even imagined then, and it is difficult to find equivalents in Israelite society. Moreover, most discussions of the doctrine of vocation usually begin with Martin Luther and the sixteenth century. Nonetheless, if one wishes to find the sources for the Reformation views on work and vocation, the Old Testament is an excellent place to start.[1] There one finds an intense focus on the meaning and purpose of work. Most important, the Old Testament presents a working God who calls His people to imitate His work. For this reason, human work that is done in the Lord takes on lasting significance (Psalm 127:1).

This chapter will begin with a narrative. The story of the Old Testament is the story of the God of Israel, shown to be the most excellent worker, and His people Israel, whom He calls to be workers like Him and whom He empowers to do His work. Having told that story, the second half of the chapter will address how this story is deeply relevant to modern workers in their occupations.

---

1 It is worth remembering that Martin Luther's background was as an interpreter of the Bible, and the interpretation of the Old Testament is very prominent in his writings.

The Story of the Working God and His Workers

I perceived that whatever God does endures forever; nothing can be added to it, nor anything taken from it. God has done it, so that people fear before Him.

Ecclesiastes 3:14

Any discussion of work and vocation in the Old Testament must begin with God Himself. From the opening verse of Genesis and through to the Last Day, God is shown to be a worker whose work endures forever. The working of God is often portrayed in vocational terms: God is described as a builder, an artisan, a potter, a farmer, a watchman, a warrior, a shepherd, a king, a physician, a father, and a husband.[2] Moreover, while divine work extends far beyond the knowledge and horizons of humanity, the Old Testament focuses on what the Lord does for the benefit of human beings. His loving work produces life, order, justice, and all other conditions for human flourishing.

The precise and orderly account of the creation in Genesis 1 underlines God's concern for His creatures and most especially for humanity. This purpose is made more explicit in Psalm 104, where we see that the waters were created to give drink (vv. 11, 13), the plants for humans to cultivate (vv. 14–15), the trees and mountains and rocks to provide habitats for the animals (vv. 17–18), the sun and moon to mark the seasons (v. 19; also Genesis 1:14), the day and night for humans to labor and rest (v. 23), the seas for ships to sail (v. 26), and all kinds of food for the continued life of all creatures (vv. 27–28). In creating humanity last, after all the preparations have been made for human life to abound, God is treating human beings as His honored guest, providing them with both blessing and vocation.[3] Having completed this

2 A few examples from the Bible can be given: God as builder (Job 38:4–7; Psalm 69:35; 127:1), artisan (Psalm 8:3; Proverbs 8:30), potter (Isaiah 29:16; 64:8; Jeremiah 18:6), farmer (Isaiah 5:1–7), watchman (Psalm 121:4), warrior (Exodus 15:3; Isaiah 42:13), shepherd (Genesis 48:15; Psalm 23; 28:9; 80:1; Isaiah 40:11; Ezekiel 34:15), king (1 Samuel 8:7; Psalm 29; 47; 93–99; Isaiah 6), physician (Exodus 15:26; Psalm 147:3; Hosea 6:1), father (Deuteronomy 8:5; 32:6; Psalm 68:5; 103:13; Proverbs 3:11–12; Isaiah 63:16; 64:8; Jeremiah 3:19; 31:9; Hosea 11:1), and husband (Isaiah 54:5–8; Jeremiah 3:20; 31:32; Ezekiel 16; Hosea 2).

3 This interpretation of God's reasons for creating the world in this order is widespread and of great antiquity in Christian writings. It dates at least as far back as the first-century Jewish thinker Philo of Alexandria in his treatise "On the Creation of the World."

very good creation, God rests, establishing the rhythm of work and rest for His creatures.

When God creates humanity in His image and likeness (Genesis 1:26–27), He creates them to be workers as He is. In the creation account, God is shown to be Creator, Orderer, and Governor of all things. Likewise, humanity is given the command to procreate (Genesis 1:28), to organize the animals by naming them (Genesis 2:19–20), and to have dominion over the earth (Genesis 1:28). This dominion is exercised directly by Adam in working and maintaining the garden (Genesis 2:15). In this way, the first man is given responsibility and purpose in loving and serving both God and His creation. That such a high honor would be given to a mere creature is a source of wonder for the Psalmist: "What is man that You are mindful of him, and the son of man that You care for him? Yet You have made him a little lower than the heavenly beings and crowned him with glory and honor. You have given him dominion over the works of Your hands; You have put all things under his feet" (Psalm 8:4–6). Moreover, everything that humanity does in vocation both is patterned after God and is ultimately the work of God in and through human beings.

But it was all broken when humanity fell into sin and distrust. One of the consequences of this fall is that human beings no longer perfectly image God and thus fail at their God-given vocations. This is acknowledged in the curses upon Adam and Eve. In the curse on Eve (Genesis 3:16), we see that human relationships, intended to be places of service and love, will be marred by selfishness and pain. In the curse on Adam (Genesis 3:17–19), we see that sin contorts meaningful work into vain toil. The book of Ecclesiastes grapples with the implications of life under the curse: "What has a man from all the toil and striving of heart with which he toils beneath the sun? For all his days are full of sorrow, and his work is a vexation. Even in the night his heart does not rest. This also is vanity" (Ecclesiastes 2:22–23). Work alienated from God is vanity, because such human accomplishments are temporary and cannot provide ultimate meaning.[4] Therefore, it is a great error

4 The term for "vanity" in Hebrew is literally "vapor"—something with little substance that lasts for only a moment.

to seek ultimate good in one's occupation or duty. Yet God continues to provide for all creatures even in this broken state, and He continues to call human beings to serve one another. In spite of human failure, ignorance, and lawlessness, God-given vocation has not vanished from the earth.

God's plan to reconcile humanity to Himself (and so redeem both human nature and human vocation from the curse) is set into motion by the covenant with Abraham. Abraham and his offspring are called to a special vocation by which God would bless all the families of the earth (Genesis 12:3; 22:18). The undoing of the ancient curse was the work of God, but it was work that He was doing by means of His chosen people. While the whole people of Israel were recipients of this high calling to be the Servant of the Lord (Exodus 4:23; Isaiah 41:8–9), not all Israelites were the same. Like a living organism, each individual Israelite had particular responsibilities and functions—whether as farmer or artisan, priest or king, parent or child—and each of these was subordinated to and contributed to the corporate vocation of Israel. Thus, even the lowliest day-laborer in Israel should see his work as the highest of callings and no less in dignity than that of the king himself.[5] In fact, the Old Testament never encourages people to seek after higher callings. Rather, they are encouraged to do the work that is set before them, and "social mobility" occurs only at the initiative of God, such as in the divine calling of judges, kings, priests, and prophets.

Vocation is most directly evident in these special offices, where we have stories of God personally calling prophets or giving the priesthood to the family of Aaron or sending His agents to anoint kings. Each of the offices of prophet, priest, and king imaged the work of God in a special way. The prophet proclaimed messages from the Lord, just as God is self-revealing, and His work is accomplished through His Word. In the priesthood, the holy presence of God was brought near to the people, as God made His people holy. Finally, the king was responsible for defending the people against dangers—both internal and external—and establishing justice so that the people could thrive. All of these

5 See Paul S. Minear, "Work and Vocation in Scripture," in *Work and Vocation: A Christian Discussion*, ed. John Oliver Nelson (New York: Harper, 1954), 48–49.

were most properly the work of God Himself, which He was accomplishing through a human representative.

To direct them in living out their corporate vocation as God's people and their individual vocations, the Israelites received the divine revelation at Sinai. The Law of Moses can be viewed as a form of vocational guidance. It showed the Israelites how they were to live as a covenant people in their daily lives. The Law was built upon the premise of Israel living in imitation of God: "You shall be holy, for I the LORD your God am holy" (Leviticus 19:2). Another principle that stands behind the Law is the love of God (Deuteronomy 6:5) and of neighbor (Leviticus 19:18).[6] If Israel fulfilled their vocation, the result would be the undoing of the curse. God would bless Israel by means of the land that He gave them, the vocations of individual Israelites living in love, and the conditions of justice that would prevail in the land. Even more, Israel would be a light to the nations, through which the justice of God would come to all humanity (Isaiah 42:1–3).

Unfortunately, Israel was never able to fully live out their vocation as the Servant of the Lord.[7] Isaiah condemns their failure in these words: "Who is blind but My servant, or deaf as My messenger whom I send? Who is blind as My dedicated one, or blind as the servant of the LORD? He sees many things, but does not observe them; his ears are open, but he does not hear" (Isaiah 42:19–20). Repeatedly, the prophets called the people to repent and return to the covenant and their God-given vocation. But Israel repeatedly chose to become like the nations around them and neglect their mission. Because theirs was a higher calling, Israel also received harsher judgment when they failed (Amos 3:2). However, even this condemnation was intended to purify Israel and draw them back to the Lord (Isaiah 1:25–26; Malachi 3:3–4).

The prophets also foretold the coming of one who would fulfill Israel's special calling as the Servant of the Lord. Isaiah records God's

6 To use one particular commandment as an example, the command to observe the Sabbath day is portrayed as both a form of imitation of the holy God who rested on the seventh day (Exodus 20:11) and as an act of compassion for those who work (Exodus 23:12; Deuteronomy 5:14–15).

7 For more on the identity of the Servant of the Lord in Isaiah, see R. Reed Lessing, *Isaiah 40–55*, Concordia Commentary (St. Louis: Concordia, 2011), 76–90.

call of this Servant to restore Israel and fulfill the vocation to reconcile humanity to God: "It is too light a thing that You should be My servant to raise up the tribes of Jacob and to bring back the preserved of Israel; I will make You as a light for the nations, that My salvation may reach to the end of the earth" (Isaiah 49:6). The prophet goes on to describe the Servant's sufferings and death that would heal humanity's sins. By this calling, the Servant would bring about justice—by making unjust people into just ones (Isaiah 52:13–53:12). In doing so, God would constitute a new Israel who would live under a new covenant (Jeremiah 31:31–34) and be the true servants of the Lord after the model of the Servant.[8] But to say much more about this, we must wait for the next chapter concerning the New Testament.

The Old Testament asserts that the Messiah fulfills not only the corporate calling of Israel but also the vocations of individual offices, such as prophet, priest, and king. He is the promised "prophet like Moses," who would faithfully proclaim God's Word and to whom Israel should listen (Deuteronomy 18:15–19). He is the true priest, mediating between God and humanity (Psalm 110:4). He is the true king, bringing about justice and peace in which humanity can flourish (Psalm 72, especially vv. 6–7). All of these Old Testament callings were types and shadows of the vocation of the Messiah, and He calls His restored people to fulfill the vocations of prophet (Numbers 11:29; Joel 2:28–29), priest (Exodus 19:5–6), and even king (Daniel 7:18, 21–22) in Him. Finally, at the Last Day, perfect justice and blessing will reign, as all work will be accomplished in the Messiah (Psalm 146:7–9; Isaiah 61:1–2). Thus, all vocation begins in God and finds completion in His Messiah.

Applying the Old Testament to Our Vocations

> I perceived that there is nothing better for them than to be joyful and to do good as long as they live; also that everyone should eat and drink and take pleasure in all his toil—this is God's gift to man.
>
> *Ecclesiastes 3:12–13*

8 The book of Isaiah uses the term "servant" twenty times in chapters 40–53, always in the singular, and eleven times in chapters 54–66, always in the plural. Isaiah is asserting that, from the work of the Servant in chapter 53, God is bringing forth many servants in His likeness.

We are part of the grand story of God and Israel. The God of the Old Testament is still the one who calls human beings to do His loving work. All human beings have God-given vocations, whether they know it or not, and these vocations are sources of divine blessing. Even more important, Jesus Christ is the true Israel of God, and accordingly those whom He calls are Israel in Him. Therefore, Christians can learn much about their vocations by looking to the story of Israel contained in the Old Testament.

This is a partial list of major vocational themes in the Old Testament. It is not meant to exhaust the topic, but rather it provides a starting point for meditating upon what the Scriptures teach us about our vocations.

God often works by means of human instruments, to whom He gives all the skills necessary to complete His work.

It is obvious from the Old Testament that God can accomplish all things by Himself without the need for human beings. After all, He created all things before human beings even existed. Nonetheless, in the story of the Old Testament, God often does His work by means of human beings. Moreover, these deeds are still understood as the work of God, even when human beings do them without any obvious miraculous interference. For example, the stories of Ezra and Nehemiah contain no explicitly supernatural events, and yet God is given full credit for building the temple and the walls of Jerusalem.[9] Similarly, in Psalm 104, God is credited with the production of bread, wine, and oil, even though these are "man-made" products (vv. 14–15). God provides the raw materials (grain, grapes, and olives), the environmental conditions (sun, rain, and soil), and the humans to cultivate, process, distribute, and market these commodities, and so it is still proper to say that God feeds all people.

When God calls human beings to do His work, He also provides all of the skills necessary to bring the task to completion. For example, when Israel was commanded to build the tabernacle, God empowered the artisans with the skill to make it excellently (Exodus 35:35). The Psalmist praises God for training him for success in war (Psalm

9 Andrew E. Steinmann, *Ezra and Nehemiah*, Concordia Commentary (St. Louis: Concordia Publishing House, 2010), 103–7.

144:1). Likewise, Moses prays that God would "establish the work of our hands" (Psalm 90:17). For these reasons, Israel is warned not to take credit for the ability that God has provided or the success that they enjoy (Deuteronomy 8:17–18). Moreover, if God provides the calling and the skill to do His will, He can also revoke it from those who fail to heed His call. This can be seen in the examples of King Saul (1 Samuel 13:13–14; 15:23) or Solomon's son Rehoboam (1 Kings 11:31), whose kingdoms were taken away because of their disobedience. It is also evident in the story of Aaron's sons Nadab and Abihu, who were destroyed for violating their offices as priests (Leviticus 10:1–2). Because all skill and authority derives from God, even the king must remember that his vocation is God's and not his own, as seen by the limitations that God places upon the royal office (Deuteronomy 17:14–20). Humility before God is appropriate for everyone in every vocation (Proverbs 15:33; Micah 6:8).

God graciously chooses the weak and lowly to accomplish His purposes, and He will not be thwarted. Hannah's song (1 Samuel 2:1–10) finds joy in the fact that God chooses to exalt the humble. He chose a childless man to be the father of His people (Abraham), a disgraced Egyptian prince to be the savior of the slaves in Egypt (Moses), and an obscure shepherd boy to be the king of Israel (David). Likewise, the prophets called by God confess their total inadequacy for the task (Exodus 3:11; 4:10; Isaiah 6:5; Jeremiah 1:6), and yet God promises that He will accomplish His will in them (Exodus 3:12; 4:11–12; Isaiah 6:6–7; Jeremiah 1:5, 7–10). All glory is the Lord's, for He accomplishes great things through lowly servants. Even when they are in exile, God continues to call His servants to do His work, as seen with Naaman's slave girl (2 Kings 5:2–3), Daniel, and Nehemiah. Human lowliness is not a burden to the working God.

The Old Testament focuses on the heart of the worker, since God desires the totality of the person.

The Old Testament is more concerned with the attitude of the worker than with the type of work that he or she does.[10] Whether one is a shepherd or a merchant or a priest, the most important issue is how one

10 Minear, "Work and Vocation," 40–41.

approaches one's work. This is well summarized in Psalm 127: "Unless the LORD builds the house, those who build it labor in vain. Unless the LORD watches over the city, the watchman stays awake in vain" (Psalm 127:1). In other words, the most relevant question for the worker is not what occupation to have but whether the Lord is doing His work when the worker is engaged in the occupation. Now, the work of God can be accomplished even when the worker does not understand or acknowledge God's role. For example, Cyrus of Persia is seen as the anointed king who accomplishes God's purposes, even though Cyrus was a pagan with no knowledge of or faith in the God of Israel (Isaiah 45:1–6). The work is no less effective or divine when done through such a person. Likewise, Jeremiah shows that God will use even the hated Babylonian regime as a source of well-being for exiled Judah, and so the Judeans should pray for Babylon's well-being (Jeremiah 29:7).

However, God wants to do more than simply accomplish His work through an individual's vocation. He wants to have the totality of that person for Himself. In God's desire that His people would belong to Him in every aspect of life, He shows interest even in the most mundane facets of their lives. This helps one to understand the Old Testament laws in all of their minute details. God gives vocational guidance that is even concerned with what food His people eat, what clothes they wear, what they think about, and what they desire and intend. Every aspect of life comes under the covenantal relationship with the Lord.[11] A similar thing can be said of Israelite wisdom literature, which is not concerned with abstractions but with the attitudes and choices of daily life.[12] Of course this includes work, for work is a major component of how one's

11 For example, in Deuteronomy the Israelites are commanded to remember the commandment to love God by making it a part of their daily routines: "You shall love the LORD your God with all your heart and with all your soul and with all your might. And these words that I command you today shall be on your heart. You shall teach them diligently to your children, and shall talk of them when you sit in your house, and when you walk by the way, and when you lie down, and when you rise. You shall bind them as a sign on your hand, and they shall be as frontlets between your eyes. You shall write them on the doorposts of your house and on your gates" (Deuteronomy 6:5–9).

12 James Bollhagen, *Ecclesiastes*, Concordia Commentary, (St. Louis: Concordia Publishing House, 2011), 24, calls the biblical wisdom approach "incarnational," in the sense that "God's grace is manifested in the bodily lives of believers, in life where it is lived."

life is spent, and it is very close to a person's heart.[13] Thus, God teaches His people to have a heart of wisdom, approaching their vocations from a place of faith.

God calls His people to give Him their very best by working with diligence.

In laying claim on the entire life of a person, God asks that one gives one's very best to God. For example, God was pleased with Abel's generous and trusting sacrifice, while He rejected Cain's half-hearted offering (Genesis 4:3–5). Likewise, God required Israel to give their first fruits to God as a sign of their priorities (Exodus 22:29–30; 23:19). In the realm of vocation, God's people are called to give Him their best by working diligently and faithfully. The book of Ecclesiastes commends us to take the vocation that is given to us and to do it well: "Whatever your hand finds to do, do it with your might" (Ecclesiastes 9:10). Furthermore, laziness or shoddy work is a sin against one's vocation and one's neighbor, and it is little better than violence and destruction (Proverbs 18:9). For this reason, the book of Proverbs is replete with warnings against lazy and lackadaisical work, and it commends hard work and dedication (Proverbs 6:6–11; 10:3–5; 12:11, 24, 27; 14:23; 20:4, 13; 21:5, 25–26; 26:13–16; 28:19). In this, humans are called to imitate God and His divine Wisdom, who works with all diligence (Proverbs 31:10–31).[14]

Work exists for the good of the neighbor.

God works on the basis of His incredible divine love, and He calls human beings to work in that same love. God loves your neighbor by using you to meet the needs of your neighbor, and you love God by loving your neighbor as yourself (Leviticus 19:18). One of the purposes of work is so that the worker would be able to give to others. We are encouraged to be diligent workers who give, not lazy ones who only take (Proverbs 21:25–26). Moreover, mundane choices must be

13 Minear, "Work and Vocation," 43.

14 This is based on the understanding that the hardworking woman of Proverbs 31 should be identified primarily with divine Wisdom, who is also portrayed in Proverbs 1–9. See Andrew Steinmann, *Proverbs*, Concordia Commentary (St. Louis: Concordia Publishing House, 2009), 634–38.

reconsidered according to the lens of vocation and responsibility to one's neighbor. For example, the Proverbs advise kings to avoid alcohol, not because drinking is evil but because a king who drinks is hindered in his vocation (Proverbs 31:4–5). The question is reframed to consider primarily the needs of the neighbor as they are met in vocation.

The call to love one's neighbor is also a call to uphold justice in the world. Justice (as the Old Testament uses the term) is the perfect harmony and order when all things are good and right, and it is the most significant prerequisite for human flourishing. It is described as the rain which causes plant-life to grow abundantly (Psalm 72:6–7). The Lord is a God of justice. He calls all authorities to establish justice within their jurisdictions so that humans may flourish. He also calls each individual to lead a life of justice. The prophetic rebuke against social injustice remains relevant today. God is opposed to every form of exploitation, capriciousness, and cruelty. Human beings are called to work in their vocations to oppose such evils for the sake of their neighbor.

Work is not the source of ultimate meaning, but it can be a penultimate source of meaning when put in its proper place.

The book of Ecclesiastes has much to say about the proper sphere for human efforts and labor (what the book calls "toil"). Ecclesiastes systematically tears down every human striving that might be a candidate for the ultimate good and source of meaning. It shows that nothing "under the sun" has permanence and ultimate significance—not wisdom, power, pleasure, or any number of other things. It even includes vocation, which produces only sorrow and vexation when one builds a life around it apart from God (Ecclesiastes 2:22–23). However, when vocation is moved out of the first place and into a subordinate position, it becomes a source of joy and contentment. In other words, Ecclesiastes teaches that vocation is a penultimate good, that is, something to be enjoyed but not something to occupy the central position in one's life. Only God can adequately stand in that place (Ecclesiastes 12:1, 13). Therefore, Ecclesiastes commends seeking penultimate meaning in vocation: "Behold, what I have seen to be good and fitting is to eat and drink and find enjoyment in all the toil with which one toils under the sun the few days of his life that God has given him, for this is his lot" (Ecclesiastes 5:18; see also 2:24–25; 9:9–10). Even more, work is called "God's gift to man" (Ecclesiastes 3:12–13). Therefore, this book reveals how to find meaning in one's labor without transforming it into an idol that will only disappoint. Vocation is one of the simple joys of a life well lived.

The worker lives under the grace of God.

All honest people can recount times when they failed at their vocation—times when they chose self-interest over love of neighbor, and times when they were less than diligent in their work, times when they made an idol out of their work. However, vocation takes place under the umbrella of God's grace, and the Old Testament reminds us that we are forgiven and that God can transform our feeble work into something valuable and enduring.

Workers do not have to bear the weight of the world on their shoulders, because God's work of providing and delivering is not contingent on their obedience. Mordecai reminded Esther of this when he told her, "For if you keep silent at this time, relief and deliverance will rise for the Jews from another place" (Esther 4:14). Numerous examples of God turning human evil into good can be found in the Bible, such as in the story of Joseph, who observed: "As for you, you meant evil against me, but God meant it for good, to bring it about that many people should be kept alive, as they are today" (Genesis 50:20). One particularly shocking instance is the story of Samson, through whom God saved Israel despite Samson's copious sins and bad intentions. God will do His gracious work with you or without you, although of course it is better for you that He does it with you.[15]

Ultimately, God's grace is sufficient even for sins against one's vocations. The story of God and Israel in the Old Testament is profoundly the story of forgiveness. God has mercy on Israel far too many times

15 Another example is Pharaoh in the story of the exodus. One way or another Pharaoh would glorify God. He would have glorified God by his obedience if he had let the people go. In actuality, he glorified God by being humbled by the great and wondrous plagues against Egypt. In this case, God accomplished His plan at the expense of Pharaoh, but Pharaoh brought judgment upon himself.

to recount here. For this reason, Micah rejoices, "Who is a God like You, pardoning iniquity and passing over transgression for the remnant of His inheritance? He does not retain His anger forever, because He delights in steadfast love" (Micah 7:18). Likewise, the Psalmist confesses, "If You, O LORD, should mark iniquities, O Lord, who could stand? But with You there is forgiveness, that You may be feared" (Psalm 130:3–4). Because the worker lives under the grace of God, it is not necessary to live in constant fear of failure and guilt over one's sins. Rather, the worker can work boldly and rest peacefully, knowing that all things are covered by the work of the Messiah.

We imitate God also in His rest.

Humankind is to imitate God in doing His work, but they are also to imitate Him in His rest (Exodus 20:11). God does not expect human beings to become workaholics who grind themselves down into exhaustion. While vocation is a beautiful gift of God that makes life richer and fuller, humanity is also meant to step away from vocation for times of rest. Even though Sabbath rest is codified in the Ten Commandments, it is not a burden but a genuine gift. The Psalmist declares, "It is in vain that you rise up early and go late to rest, eating the bread of anxious toil; for He gives to His beloved sleep" (Psalm 127:2). Moreover, our times of rest and recreation are also a foreshadowing of the great Sabbath rest that the Lord has prepared for all of those who serve Him.

Conclusion

> What is man that You are mindful of him, and the son of man that You care for him? Yet You have made him a little lower than the heavenly beings and crowned him with glory and honor. You have given him dominion over the works of Your hands; You have put all things under his feet.
>
> *Psalm 8:4–6*

It is a holy mystery that the almighty God has chosen lowly human beings, so that His eternal works might be accomplished in their temporary labors. In doing so, God transfigures one's toil in a cursed world into an expression of divine love for one's neighbor. Work is a profound responsibility and privilege, and its success is guaranteed by the promise of the Lord alone. This is already evident in the Old Testament, and it will become only clearer in the full revelation of the Messiah in the New Testament.

VOCATION AND WORK IN THE NEW TESTAMENT

CJ Armstrong

Rev. CJ Armstrong, PhD, is Professor of History and Theology at Concordia University Irvine. He also serves as associate pastor at Holy Trinity Lutheran Church in Hacienda Heights, CA. He has published with Concordia Publishing House the General Epistles *volume of the Reformation Heritage Bible Commentary (2014) and was translator for* Lutheranism vs. Calvinism: The Classic Debate at the Colloquy of Montbéliard 1586 *(2017).*

Called to Serve in the Various Realms

Vocation and work are distinct. Vocation as we understand it in this study concretely defines the various roles God calls one to fulfill in accordance with his or her relationships with neighbor. We discharge our obligations to family members, people who are gifts of God in Christ, whom we variously obey and serve, guide and teach, love and honor. We discharge our duties to fellow community members, people who are gifts of God in Christ, in countless interactions in the public square, observing laws and statutes, ensuring peace with neighbors, engaging or refraining from social action including political activity, voting, and when called to do so, judging and acquitting, for example in jury service. We discharge our responsibilities to the church, people who are gifts of God in Christ, in attending to public worship, intercession for the saints and the world, faithful stewardship of gifts and offerings, and gladly hearing and learning God's Word and responding in service to neighbor.

When we talk like this, we confess that "vocation" is not a singular destiny, a hidden inner calling, a mystical mission, any more than it is a personal sense of one's purpose in life. While language that seeks to reinforce the significance of individual professions is current in a variety of fields (e.g., "You know, teaching is really a *calling*"; "I really feel *called* to this profession"), we treat vocation more accurately when we realize instead that it describes the state that God has truly, externally, called people to in relation to their neighbors in these various realms, institutions, or, as the Latin-loving theologians of the past called them, *ordines*. The *ordo* of family, of state, of church—all the *ordines*—are understood as spheres of activity in which one individual is called to serve various people in various ways, and therefore one has as many vocations as one has neighbors to serve. The same woman is mother to her children, sister to her siblings, wife to her husband; she is citizen of her local municipality as well as her state, region, and national government; and she may also be church member, usher, committee member, education board director, and funeral reception coordinator. The reason we take time to think about all those roles overlapping in the one person is first to conceive of the many, many hats one person is always asked to wear—and we would remark that we don't usually take one off before putting another one on!—and second to note that in none of these examples have we once brought up the *job*, the *occupation*, the *work* that this person gets paid for. One does not *choose* one's vocations. Vocation is objective at its root: *you* are the object of *God's* calling, not the other way round.

Human Activity Sanctified in Christ's Humanity

In regard to vocation and work, the New Testament record indicates above all that in Jesus Christ human activity is sanctified. That is to say, human activity has been made holy, set apart for special use and consideration, elevated, made the concern of God Himself, a state of affairs effected by no less than the central mystery of faith, the incarnation of the Son of God, whom God sent forth, as Paul says in Galatians 4, when the time had fully come, "born of woman, born under the law, to redeem those who were under the law" (vv. 4–5). Christ entered the world as a human being, a man in the flesh, and in so doing sanctifies all flesh. God did not enter the world in Christ to save human beings from their bodies; He came in a body to save them from their sin.

What does the centrality of recognizing and confessing the embodied, incarnate Lord Jesus have to do with vocation and work?

It reminds us that whatever task we do with our embodied reason and all our embodied senses, whatever work we perform with our body's eyes, ears, and all our members, and in fact whatever work we put our embodied minds to is sanctified, set apart for special purpose in the Lord's economy. The incarnation of the Son of God suggests that humanity itself and human enterprise are significant to God, who has a purpose for it—though this purpose may well be invisible to eyes of flesh and must be seen with eyes of faith.

This is why such work need not be elevated in the world's opinion in order to be acceptable, not to mention honored, by God. The witness of the New Testament prophet John the Baptist is sufficient to demonstrate the point. Besides the general command of charity he gives to the crowds of repentant seekers at the Jordan—"Whoever has two tunics is to share with him who has none, and whoever has food is to do likewise" (Luke 3:11)—the evangelist records his advice to two specific groups identified by their *occupations*: tax collectors and soldiers. These professions were hardly considered laudable, acceptable, or honorable in all circles, particularly those with religious scruples concerned with the identity of God's people in first-century Judea who would exist in an uncomfortable, if not adversarial, position with such public figures who appeared not to serve their interests. Both tax collectors and military men were agents of Roman authority, a reminder of the political subjection of Jerusalem and its environs, the eastern reaches of an empire whose center was more than a thousand miles away. Yet John does not vilify the professions of these repentant petitioners; indeed, in answering them he underscores the dignity of the work they do, even as he commands good works in keeping with repentance: "Tax collectors also came to be baptized and said to him, 'Teacher, what shall we do?' And he said to them, 'Collect no more than you are authorized to do.' Soldiers also asked him, 'And we, what shall we do?' And he said to them, 'Do not extort money from anyone by threats or by false accusation, and be content with your wages'" (Luke 3:12–14).

Assessing the message the New Testament would teach us in regard to vocation and work could proceed from this (rather remarkable) example to catalog the various occupations described in Holy Writ, which a quick scan reveals to include, besides tax collector and soldier, such varied jobs as miller, fisherman, herdsman, farmer, public official, soldier, scribe, priest, smith (and craftsman in general), tanner, tentmaker, textile manufacturer, innkeeper, sailor, physician, teacher, tradesman, entertainer, banker, stonemason (and builder in general)—and we would be invited to fill in the interstices with an almost limitless number of real people whose occupations supplied, processed, retailed, consumed, and otherwise bought and sold the labor of these real people, who functioned in a society stratified and regulated by factors of relative wealth, class, and patronage. Moreover, throughout all of these occupations, overtly expressed or implied, the New Testament assumes, as does the entire record of first-century Mediterranean literature, the extension of that patronizing economic system that we know as the institution of slavery. A study attempting to embrace such a scope would be too complex to treat faithfully in a book, much less a chapter. Assessing the New Testament message about work could on the other hand trace just the commands about occupational activity to extract some pithy or inspirational verses to deliver God's counsel in refrigerator-magnet fashion, such as Colossians 3:23: "Whatever you do, work heartily, as for the Lord and not for men!" Simple—and great advice!—but the convenience of a sentiment so succinct would tempt us to isolate the occupations too quickly, ignoring the fact that they are a subset of the wider world of vocations described in the New Testament that include more than the work one does for a living, vocations such as mother, father, citizen, and neighbor.

Vocation: A Life Sanctified to Serve Neighbor

A broader approach is to consider that vocation is about service to neighbor, the sanctified life. The most replete teaching on the subject in the New Testament is undoubtedly the doctrinally rich paraenetic sections of Paul's letters. It is helpful in this short space, therefore, to turn to Romans 12–15 to consider the framework of New Testament thinking when it comes to vocation and work.[1] The broader framework

1 Doctrinal passages on the nature of vocation that parallel Paul's teaching in Romans 12–15 (and should therefore be considered when thinking about a New Testament theology of work) include 1 Corinthians 12–14, Ephesians 5–6, Colossians 3–4, 2 Thessalonians 3, 1 Timothy 5, Titus 3, and 1 Peter 2–3.

of Paul's letter to the Romans envisions Christ the Redeemer as the substitutionary sacrifice acceptable to God on behalf of all humanity; in Romans, Paul argues that Christ is the new Adam, come into the world to undo the fall into sin perpetrated by the old Adam, whose sin taints all flesh. In Christ, therefore, humanity is reborn through His death and resurrection, which sanctifies humanity, individual human beings, and individual and collective human activity. In the second half of his letter, the apostle demonstrates the practical implications of this thesis that unfold for those who have faith in Christ. Broadly speaking, these implications are bound up with obligations to neighbor in the various realms we have described, or, in a word, vocation (of which a person's occupational activity or work is but one example).

Living Sacrifices

To the sinner who has died and risen in Christ through baptism, through confession and faith, through trusting that he or she is dead to sin and alive to God in Christ, Romans 12 addresses the "now what?" question. The Christian is saved by grace, justified before God through faith in Christ, no longer under law but rather under grace, with no one to condemn the one who is in Christ Jesus—all good news! Now how shall I live? The apostle Paul offers this answer: "Present your bodies as a living sacrifice, holy and acceptable to God, which is your spiritual worship" (Romans 12:1).

Living sacrifice that is holy and acceptable to God does not entail some sort of supernatural empowerment to be a different kind of lawyer, doctor, mechanic, or mom, distinguished by an urgency to go above and beyond the regular duties of those roles, on a mission (overt or secret) to evangelize. Living sacrifice that is holy and acceptable to God is not driven by guilt to consider that God is watching, so you better look busy, any more than it is driven by pious determination to behave in ways alien to the role in question. Living sacrifice that is holy and acceptable to God follows the Christ whose sacrifice was accomplished out of love for sinners. In that order of love, Christians follow Christ within their vocations, whether in the home, in society, in church, or in the workplace. A popular misunderstanding of the Christian faith and Christian vocation, in spite of the good intentions from which it no doubt springs, would assume that the call of the Christian is actively to supplement one's vocational activity with man-made notions of piety, what the human imagination may conceive of as holy rather than what God has revealed in His Word. "Since I'm a Christian I shouldn't judge people, so I will refuse to serve on a jury" is as misguided a conclusion as those that sixteenth-century church reformers disputed when dealing with monks and nuns who had been taught that "serving the church is a more honorable calling than raising a family" and other such traditions of men. Attempting to add to what God reveals about human freedom and responsibility ultimately ends by burdening consciences with the idea that we must do something special in order to please God. No. Spiritual worship, living sacrifice, originates with confidence that, instead, God has done something special *for us* in Christ, indeed, that *His* sacrifice sanctifies the Christian entirely, whatever his or her roles, whatever his or her callings in the world. Living sacrifice that is pleasing to God means following Christ in all the realms to which He has called the Christian, including professional employment.

When Paul talks in the language of "living sacrifices," he is aware of the oxymoron. Worshipers of the Jewish faith knew well the institution of sacrifice performed according to the Lord's command at the temple in Jerusalem; first-century Gentiles of the Mediterranean basin worshiped many gods and frequented their shrines and temples with sacrifices of animal victim bodies as well. Pagan worship in the ancient Mediterranean was rather transactional: I give to a god in order that it may give back to me, implying that the divine powers can be bargained with, that one can make a deal with them, give them something to satisfy the question "what's in it for me?" In our own time and place, although we do not perform animal sacrifices, we may nevertheless be prone to think that our offerings somehow fill a need that God has, serving as a bargaining chip in our favor, whether the offerings of our treasures in a church offering plate or a charitable contribution in society, whether a good deed motivated by an attempt to justify oneself before God or one driven by a desire to impress other people. The New

Testament, however, teaches us that what God requires in the way of good works has little to do with His need but rather the needs of others. Christ's parable of the sheep and the goats (Matthew 25:31–46) illustrates this profoundly: the goats on the judge's left are dumbfounded to hear that their pity was misplaced ("when did we . . . not minister to You?" [Matthew 25:44]). The judge's universal verdict is "Truly, I say to you, as you did it to one of the least of these My brothers, you did it to Me" (Matthew 25:40), or not, in the case of those who ignore the needs of the neighbor. A New Testament theology teaches this about good works, including the work we perform in all of our callings. God does His creative and redemptive work *through* people, *for* people. His secret agents for performing His creative and redemptive work in the world are hidden behind the masks of people who, as they work, are for the most part unaware that the one they serve is Christ ("When did we see you hungry and feed You?" etc. [Matthew 25:37–39]), who would say with those in another of Jesus' parables that they "are unworthy servants; we have only done what was our duty" (Luke 17:10). God's incarnational work of salvation for the cosmos was accomplished once for all time in the sacrificial death of Christ on the cross (John 3:16; 19:30; 1 Peter 3:18); God's continuing work of salvation for individual people in time is accomplished by Him incarnationally, through real people doing work according to their callings, no longer as a sacrifice for sins but as living sacrifices (Romans 12:1). According to Paul, God's plans are in direct opposition to the world's notions of transactional peace with God through our own efforts and its pattern of pride in one's own dignity, worth, and work. This is why the apostle continues by beseeching the body of Christ no longer to be conformed to the pattern of this world, but to "be transformed by the renewal of your mind" (Romans 12:2). The righteous ones of Christ's Matthew 25 parable are told that the good work they do, they do for God, and this work is identical with the work they do for people. Paul's "renewal of your mind" implies among other things an invitation to see reality the way that God sees it: that the work we do is God's way of working in the world, and that the neighbor we serve in our work is Christ Himself, under the masks of those in need.

Serving the Need

Those in need—who are these people? They are everyone around you in an overwhelming network of interdependency. The "one of the least of these My brothers" (Matthew 25:40) is not served by extraordinary super-saints who organize their time in the day to spend one hour visiting a prison, another finding a thirsty person to offer water to, yet another to sew clothing for those who are naked, and so on every day of the week. The needy, interdependent objects of God's creative and redemptive work are served in reality by the many hands of the many agents of God's work under the masks of the farmer, the harvester, the processor, the warehouser, the distributor, the retailer, the family provider, and the food preparer in order to feed the hungry children in your house with a loaf of bread at mealtime. The textile manufacturer, the entire staff of the factory, and in their contributions even the fashion designer and company stockholders, not to mention the web team and driver for Amazon.com, get the naked clothed so moms and dads and teachers and principals can rest easy in the dress codes they agree to at their government-supported middle school. God is at work at every stage of all these instances. The invitation of the New Testament is to see that the work we get to do, whether in our business or our home, our church or our local political assemblies, is God's work in the world, and we are His agents, both receiving what we need from Him under the masks He chooses to employ and serving our neighbors under the mask of the work before us, whatever our station in life happens to be at any moment.

The renewal of the mind makes your profession, your work, look entirely new. The renewal of our minds, seeing things the way God sees them (which is seeing through the eyes of faith in Christ), frees us to see that our society is ordered by Him in order that He may accomplish miraculous work, even if that work appears mundane on the surface. The dignity of even the most mundane tasks—raising a family, political organization, professional activity—rests in the Christ who sees a world in need and sends you there to answer your callings. Notice how this New Testament vision of vocation is rather more rich than the world's simplistic advice to follow your passion or to find work that you love so you won't ever work a day in your life or some such platitude. Sometimes you are not passionate. It doesn't matter if you are never passionate! Sometimes work just needs to be done. The New Testament teaches that this also is spiritual worship and elevated, sanctified, even if it does not find worldly rewards or get celebrated with fireworks. Rather, it concretizes vocation in the work we find before us, whatever our station in life, because when we do our duty, we are filling a great need, despite our feelings about it. You don't have to be thrilled to go to work. God is thrilled for you, even if you are not!

The renewal of the mind that Paul refers to in Romans 12:2, seeing that God is at work in your work, is matched by the apostle's continuing argument, where he celebrates the diversity of gifts that enable that work. Gifts are given, and God is the giver. God the Holy Spirit distributes these gifts to be used (Romans 12:6); no one is sufficient in themselves, we are all interdependent, and so the renewal of the mind includes also the admonition that one not "think of himself more highly than he ought to think" but rather "think with sober judgment, each according to the measure of faith that God has assigned" (Romans 12:3). The apostle reinforces the fact that God is the one empowering Christians for the tasks before them, and that the gifts He delivers are sufficient to serve in every station, because we do not rely on only our own individual God-given gifts but also the gifts He distributes to others. The New Testament consistently underscores this ethos of service to the needs facing us in all situations, which is why it is no surprise that Paul summarizes the attitude that drives the work of a Christian in the world with one word: love. So imagine for a moment that the Lord is speaking this admonition to you in regard to your work life, your professional life: "Let love be genuine. . . . Love one another with brotherly affection" (Romans 12:9–10). Since love is the mode of service for the work we do in all of our vocations, Paul can boldly admonish Christians considering their calling in relationship with others. How would you think differently, how would you speak and act differently, how would you work differently if this advice characterized not only your family life and your church life but your work life too? "Be patient in tribulation. . . . Contribute to the needs of the saints and seek to show hospitality. Bless those who persecute you. . . . Live in harmony with one another. Do not be haughty, but associate with the lowly. Never be wise in your own sight. . . . Never avenge yourselves. . . . Do not be overcome by evil, but overcome evil with good" (Romans 12:12–14, 16, 19, 21).

Love and Work

Paul continues by revealing that love and honor characterize the Christian's relationship with authorities as well, even in the state. Obedience to a chain of command is not a monolithic virtue; the apostle rather admonishes his audience to see that love and honor guide our relationship with the state: "he is God's servant for your good, . . . an avenger who carries out God's wrath on the wrongdoer. Therefore one must be in subjection, not only to avoid God's wrath but also for the sake of conscience. . . . For the authorities are ministers of God" (Romans 13:4–6). This is masks-of-God talk once again, and lest we think it pertains only to the Christian's relationship with the state, or that we are off track with theological extrapolations from the point, Paul expressly concludes: "pay to all what is owed to them: taxes to whom taxes are owed, revenue to whom revenue is owed, respect to whom respect is owed, honor to whom honor is owed" (Romans 13:7). He continues the trope of debt and payment in a universal statement that embraces all vocations when he underscores the mode by which to discharge all obligations: "Owe no one anything, except to love each other, for the one who loves another has fulfilled the law" (Romans 13:8). Paul is saying do your duty (to all!), but you can never love the neighbor too much—a debt, an obligation in vocation, that can never be fully discharged.

Christian love and honor in our work and our professions is in direct opposition to the acquisitiveness that characterizes the sinful nature, the temptation to greed that the New Testament expressly warns against. Wealth, money, property, power—Scripture looks at all of these goods as gifts of God, and as gifts, to be received with gratitude and used for the benefit of the other. The New Testament authors are entirely in harmony in suggesting we hold on to such gifts with a loose hand, from the evangelists who record Christ commanding some to sell all they have and follow Him to Paul's admonition to Timothy that "harmful desires . . . plunge people into ruin and destruction. For the love of money is a root of all kinds of evils. It is through this craving that some have wandered away from the faith and pierced themselves with many pangs" (1 Timothy 6:9–10). Hebrews 13:5 echoes Paul's sentiment with the command, "Keep your life free from love of money, and be content with what you have, for He has said, 'I will never leave you nor forsake you.'" Work directed toward acquisition as an end in itself is the road to idolatry and destruction, as illustrated in Christ's parable of the rich fool (Luke 12:13–21), which He introduces with the warning, "Take care, and be on your guard against all covetousness, for one's life does not consist in the abundance of his possessions" (Luke 12:15). Lording over the inferior, blissful ignorance of others' need, patronizing in order to reinforce one's superiority: these are the opposite of the loving ethos of service Paul's law of love demands. Do you see your work as service to others? If you lead or employ others, do you see your role as a superior as an opportunity to assist, aid, and benefit others in their service? Do you see that your diligent labor is worth far more to the God who works in it "for the least of these My brothers" than the value of the paltry sum you sell it for in exchange for a stipend, a salary, or a wage?

If "love is the fulfilling of the law" (Romans 13:10), then the neighbor served in our work and our professions is best served when we listen to Paul's further admonition: "We who are strong have an obligation to bear with the failings of the weak, and not to please ourselves. Let each of us please his neighbor for his good, to build him up" (Romans 15:1–2). Here the examples of a parent loving his or her child for the child's good, a friend counseling a friend for the good of the other, a judge distributing justice for the good of the individual and the group in need, all find an analogy in the weaker and the stronger in the workplace as well. In seeking the good of the other, the worker is discharging his or her vocation as did Christ—who "did not please Himself" (Romans 15:3), who "came not to be served but to serve" (Matthew 20:28).

Conclusion

The center of the New Testament is a worker, Jesus Christ, the incarnate Son of God, whose humanity sanctifies human activity. Faith in His saving work is faith in His human flesh dying, His human flesh rising from the grave, His human flesh ascending to the right hand of God, and further, His human flesh enlivening those who trust in Him, who are called His body. This body, with all its parts, is active in the world as a priesthood—not individual priests, but rather an entire priesthood proclaiming God's saving work in Christ and acting to "work out your own salvation" (Philippians 2:12) by working in the world. This means not that human beings make a contribution to their salvation but that they respond to the salvation wrought in the person and work of Christ by contributing to the needs of their neighbors.

Professional activity, occupation, work, is not the limit of vocation. But the New Testament wisdom regarding vocation does inspire the Christian's work in fields that he or she is paid for, no less than those services for which he or she receives no monetary reward. The power that enlivens the Christian's work is the work done by Christ on his or her behalf; indeed the work done has its origin in the Worker, Christ (1 Peter 2:4–10), and Christ is ultimately the one worked for (Colossians 3:23–24; Matthew 25:40), that it all be Christ. You, worker, are set apart for good purpose. Your work is elevated; it is cosmically significant in the Christ "who works in you, both to will and to work for His good pleasure" (Philippians 2:13).

VOCATION, WORK, AND HUMAN FLOURISHING

David W. Loy

Rev. David W. Loy, PhD, is Professor of Philosophy, Theology, and Ethics and Dean of Christ College at Concordia University Irvine. He is also the founding director of the FaithWorks Center at Concordia. He edited C. F. W. Walther's American-Lutheran Pastoral Theology; *his currently scholarly research centers on the doctrine of vocation. Before coming to Concordia, he served as pastor of Zion Lutheran Church in Bolivar, MO.*

Introduction

Your work is important to God. That is true whether your work is preaching the Gospel or repairing cars or preparing financial statements or caring for the sick. Your work is important to God because it serves those whom He created and whom He redeemed through the life, death, and resurrection of His Son, Jesus. He wishes for us human beings to have abundant life—to flourish—and He works through His Son, Jesus Christ, and through us human beings to bring about our flourishing. This chapter will outline how the Christian teachings about vocation and work inform the lives of professionals, through whom God works to help people in this world thrive and flourish.

Two Kingdoms

Does God, in fact, care whether cars get repaired or financial statements get prepared or the sick get care? The answer is yes, and the doctrine (or teaching) of the two kingdoms helps explain why. This teaching describes two ways in which God our heavenly Father distributes His rich gifts so that we human beings can flourish despite our sin. On the one hand (the right hand, so to speak), human flourishing apart from a trust-filled relationship with the Father is always incomplete. God created us to relate to and rely on Him. Without that relationship and that childlike trust in the God who created us, we live impoverished lives. This is a statement about the objective condition of the human being apart from faith in God, not a statement about the individual's subjective experience of well-being. It is possible for human beings who do not relate to and rely on God through Christ as their gracious heavenly Father to experience their lives as full, satisfying, and complete. Yet if we were created for fellowship with God, then such a subjective experience is incomplete. Human beings do not flourish in the fullest sense of the word without relating to and relying on the God who created them.

According to the Bible, it is only through Christ that we human beings fully relate to and rely on the God who created us (John 14:6; Acts 4:12). An analogy may be helpful here. It is possible to relate to a friend as if the individual were the person you wish he or she would be. Yet in doing so, you fail to relate to the person as he or she is. You are no longer relating to the person but to your idea of the person. You are not accepting your friend on his or her own terms but attempting to create a relationship only on your terms. The result will be alienation. It is much the same when we seek to relate to God apart from Christ: we are seeking to establish a relationship on our own terms, with our idea of god. The result will be alienation. Only through Christ can we relate to and rely on God as He wishes, because through Christ we know God as He wishes to be known: as the God who not only shows us our sin but who also shows us His love by forgiving us for the sake of Christ. This is God's right-hand work: to reconcile us to Himself through Christ (Romans 5:11; 2 Corinthians 5:19) so that we "may have life and have it abundantly" (John 10:10)—so that we may flourish.

Yet our gracious Father also distributes a different kind of riches so that we flourish in a different sense. He created us as particular kinds of creatures. We are physical beings who need food to sustain us (Genesis 1:29; 9:3). We are social creatures for whom it is not good to be alone (Genesis 2:18–25), creatures who can invent new ways to use the products of the earth to sustain and protect ourselves (Genesis 4:2, 20, 22), who can create beautiful works of visual and musical art to provoke thought or bring joy to others (Genesis 4:21), who can teach and learn and reflect on what we have learned (Genesis 3:2–3). We are creatures who can organize our efforts to accomplish together what we cannot accomplish alone (Genesis 11:1–4 provides an unfortunate example). We are embodied, social, political creatures.[1] We cannot flourish in the full sense of the word unless we enjoy the kinds of goods appropriate to our nature as embodied, social, political creatures. We need food. We need intimate relationships with friends, family, and spouses. We need others to contribute to our well-being, and we need to contribute to theirs. It is precisely these things that God provides out of His riches in His left-hand rule (Genesis 8:22; Psalm 145:15; Matthew 5:45).

The so-called estates or *ordines*—church, government, and household—are the arenas in which God provides what we need to flourish in every sense of the word. God uses the church to proclaim the good news about Christ and administer the sacraments in order to bring us back into a trusting, loving relationship with Him through the work of the Holy Spirit. He uses government and household to provide the conditions and goods necessary for us to flourish as embodied, social, and political creatures. In the best possible world, all people would trust their heavenly Father through Christ and would therefore love their neighbors to the point of self-sacrifice. No one would be in need. However, that is not the world we live in, because we human beings have fallen away from loving God and loving one another perfectly. This raises a question for Christians: how shall we follow Jesus in an imperfect world?

Vocation

One response is that we should Christianize the world. Our calling is to ensure that everyone who lives with us in society—and particularly those who hold positions of authority in government, business, the arts, and so on—also follow Jesus.[2] This line of thought certainly captures an important point from the Scriptures: that God calls Christians to bear witness to the hope they have in Christ (e.g., Matthew 28:19–20;

1 By "political creatures," I mean that we negotiate over power and authority when we organize ourselves to act together. We are not like bees and ants, who are social, but whose social hierarchy is static. This definition is slightly different from Aristotle's at *Politics* I.1253a1.

2 See, for example, Dallas Willard and Gary Black Jr., *The Divine Conspiracy Continued: Fulfilling God's Kingdom on Earth* (New York: HarperOne, 2014).

Acts 1:8; 1 Peter 3:15). Sharing the good news about Jesus Christ is not optional. At the same time, this line of thought is not without dangers. It suggests that the Christian life must be supported and sustained by social and political institutions and is therefore deficient if lived among people who are not Christian. Yet that is not what the Bible says. The apostles did not locate the essence or sufficiency of Christian life in the attempt to transform their culture. They located it in Christ. What drove them was not a desire to Christianize Israel or the Roman Empire but simply the burning conviction that no human flourishes fully apart from Christ. They preached because they loved those to whom they preached with a love kindled by the Spirit.

A second response is that we should withdraw from sinful society into smaller, more intimate, more faithful communities. Medieval monasticism, the Reformation-era Anabaptists movements, and contemporary calls for Christians to form their own communities instead of reforming society all grow out of impulses like this one.[3] What the impulse gets right is that Christians ought not live alone, as if our faith were a merely private matter sustained by our own willpower in the face of overwhelming opposition (Acts 2:42; Colossians 3:16; Hebrews 10:25). Christians need one another. As we confess our faith to one another, we strengthen one another in that confession. As we pray for one another, we minister to one another with God's love and mercy. As we confess our sins to one another and forgive one another in Christ's name, we share Jesus. As we live lives of love, we spur one another on to good works. We need fellow Christians. At the same time, neither Jesus nor His apostles called the earliest Christians to minimize the amount of contact they had with unbelievers. Paul's discussion of meat sacrificed to idols in 1 Corinthians 8 presupposes that Christians continued to interact with unbelievers in the everyday business of Greco-Roman life: work, weddings, and the like. John the Baptist's answer to the tax collectors and soldiers in Luke 3 presupposes that the repentant could continue to serve in their current occupations.[4]

3 One example is Rod Dreher, *The Benedict Option: A Strategy for Christians in a Post-Christian Age* (New York: Sentinel, 2017).

4 For a discussion of this passage, see CJ Armstrong's essay "Vocation and Work in the New Testament" in this volume.

Why? Because the Christian faith is a matter of the heart, as the Lutheran reformers said—a heart reconciled to God in Christ, filled with faith created by God the Holy Spirit, and moved to loving action by the Father's love for us. The Christian loves where he or she sees need. And the Christian sees need first and foremost close to home: in family, among neighbors, and at work. From there the awareness of need expands to the entire town or city, to the county and state, to the nation, and even to the entire world. What does it mean to follow Jesus in an imperfect world? It means to see the needs of those around us and to meet them as we are able, just as our heavenly Father meets our needs. "We love because He first loved us" (1 John 4:19).

That is vocation. It is the call to follow Jesus where you see need by meeting those needs with your time, talents, and treasure. Speaking sociologically, we might say that it involves meeting needs that arise among those with whom you relate in your particular social roles. If you are a spouse, you are called to follow Jesus by meeting your spouse's needs. If you are a parent, you are called to follow Jesus by meeting your children's needs. If you are a neighbor, a citizen, a human being, you are called to follow Jesus by meeting the needs of your neighbors, your fellow citizens, and any human being you meet—within the constraints of your God-given capacities. Vocation is therefore first of all local.[5] It is a call to follow Christ within the specific relationships one has here and now.

The definition of vocation offered here might seem to apply only to Christians, since vocation is defined as "the call to follow Jesus where you see need by meeting those needs with your time, talents, and treasure." Yet it is clear that non-Christians live in the same sorts of social roles as Christians. They render the same kinds of care as non-Christians in those social roles. Can they be said to have vocations? If "vocation" refers to heeding Christ's call to follow Him, then non-Christians do not have vocations, since they do not believe that Christ has called

5 Cf. Martin Luther's discussion of parenting in his "Treatise on Good Works" (1520), *Luther's Works* 44:85: "For what are the hungry, the thirsty, the naked, the sick, the alien if not the souls of your own children?"

them to follow Him.[6] On the other hand, if "vocation" refers to the call to serve our neighbor in our various social roles, then non-Christians do have vocations. And in fact, Christ does call all people to love their neighbors. He does so not only through the Bible or preaching but also through the needs of our neighbors. People who see the needs of those around them and seek to meet those needs—whether parents who care for their children, people who go into the caring professions to help others, or even citizens who vote for policies they believe will help people in their communities—these people are responding to the call that Christ issues through the needs of others. However, what non-Christians do not believe or know is that Christ, the Son of God who died and rose to redeem them from sin, death, and the devil, is the One who is calling them. From a Lutheran perspective, one might say that they hear the call, but they do not fully discern the voice of the One who calls them.[7]

Work

While all our vocations are important, this chapter focuses specifically on the vocation of work. Work is more complicated than we might think. It has individual, economic, social, and political aspects. The individual aspects are easiest to see: individuals work to survive, to enjoy good things, to interact with others, to feel satisfaction, to help others. We work, most basically, to obtain the food, clothing, and shelter necessary to survive. But given the chance, most human beings will continue working even after obtaining the bare necessities. We work because we want to enjoy better things than we currently have—food that is more nutritious or more full of taste, better opportunities for our children, and so forth. Some people work in order to socialize with others; in fact, many people report that social interaction is significant part of what makes work satisfying. Some people choose specific jobs for the sense of satisfaction they receive. They can look at what they have done

6 See Einar Billing, *Our Calling: A Statement of the Relationship of Christian Faith and Christian Living*, trans. Conrad Bergendoff (Rock Island, IL: Augustana Press, 1955) and Gustaf Wingren, *Luther on Vocation*, trans. Carl C. Rasmussen (Evansville, IN: Ballast Press, 1994), ch. 1.

7 For a fuller discussion of this question, see David W. Loy, "Called by Whom and How? Reflections on the Structure of Vocation," *Concordia Journal* 49, no. 1 (Winter 2023): 35–46.

and feel good about the skill they brought to bear, the solutions they devised to problems, the joy they got simply from focusing on the process. Finally, some people work in specific jobs in order to help others. Those in nursing, medicine, and allied health professions often express this motivation for entering their chosen fields, as do students in ministry-related programs.

Yet work is not merely about the individual who is working. The benefits the individual receives are very real gifts from our gracious Father, but other people benefit from the individual's work as well. That is to say, work has an economic aspect.[8] God uses the work I do to meet the needs of someone else, and He uses the work other people do to meet my needs and the needs of yet other people, and in this way He provides everything I (and you and everyone else) need for daily life. How my labor comes to benefit you and how your labor comes to benefit me varies across time and place. In Martin Luther's late medieval context, most products did not travel very far, and their producers might well have face-to-face relationships with their purchasers. Dr. Luther ate fish that Mrs. Luther and her employees raised on the family farm just outside of town, and Mrs. Luther dealt directly with the craftsman in Wittenberg to purchase the equipment needed to run the fish farm. The fish I eat traveled much farther, and neither I nor my wife has a personal relationship with anyone in the long chain of people who brought the fish to the local grocery store. Yet even in our contemporary economy, where the people who brought the fish to my local grocery store remain largely unknown to me or one another, I nevertheless benefit from their labor—and they benefit indirectly from my labor, since it enables me to purchase the fish in the first place.

Adam Smith's well-known invisible hand helps explain how the needs of individual human beings generate a complex network of labor exchange in which people's needs are met—that is, how human need generates an economy.[9] Immanuel Kant's notion of humanity's "unsocial sociability" likewise helps explain how people who do

8 See Gene Edward Veith, *Working for Our Neighbor: A Lutheran Primer on Vocation, Economics, and Ordinary Life* (Grand Rapids, MI: Christian's Library Press, 2016), especially ch. 6.

9 Adam Smith, *An Inquiry into the Nature and Causes of the Wealth of Nations*, book IV, chapter 2.

not necessarily care about one another or even want to live with one another nevertheless enter society in order to have their needs met, thereby meeting others' needs as well.[10] Martin Luther offers a more theologically informed viewpoint. Not everyone works out of love for neighbor, as God calls us to do, but God nevertheless uses each person's need to push him or her into the network of exchange, thus using the individual's need and/or labor to provide for the needs of all God's human creations.[11] In fact, in our complex modern economy, the need and labor of hundreds of millions of individuals across six continents (or even seven, if we count researchers living in Antarctica) interact in such a unique way that people not directly related to any given economic exchange may nevertheless experience significant benefits from it. For example, if well-to-do consumers in a town demand a healthier selection of food in the local grocery store, the entire community will benefit from the availability of the new foods.

At the same time, our modern economy is full of imperfect human beings, some of whom show remarkably little respect for the people around them. And even when we human beings act in good faith, markets can have unintended negative consequences for certain groups, leaving those groups worse off. For example, well-to-do neighborhoods often have the economic power and political clout to prevent undesirable (and potentially dangerous) development near them. Impoverished neighborhoods often lack the clout to do so, leaving them to bear burdens of pollution or soil contamination from activities that produce benefits for other neighborhoods. There is no specific bad actor in this case who is seeking to harm another group, but one group nevertheless ends up being harmed as communities, families, and individual human beings negotiate the complex network of need and labor that constitutes our modern economy. When bad actors enter the scene, matters become much worse—for example, when a company disposes of hazardous waste without proper environmental remediation despite the cost to the surrounding neighbors and ecosystems. It takes an entity with significant power to hold bad actors

10 Immanuel Kant, "Idea for a University History with a Cosmopolitan Intent," fourth thesis.

11 See Veith, *Working for Our Neighbor*, ch. 6, and Wingren, *Luther on Vocation*, 27–28, 36.

accountable, discourage actors from acting badly in the first place, and mitigate the unintended harms of the markets. It takes a government. Thus, our work has a political component as well, because our work takes place within the context of our common life together and because it can so negatively affect the shape of our common life together. That is one reason God instituted governments: because we human beings are sinful, and even a government composed of sinful human beings can keep the sin of other human beings in check (Romans 13:1–7), especially if the government itself is kept in check by constitutional checks and balances as well as the opinion of its citizens.[12]

So, from the human perspective, work is labor engaged in to satisfy certain needs or desires by producing goods or offering services that meet the needs or desires of other people and that are exchanged for goods or services those other people offer as well. From a theological perspective, work is the labor that God elicits from us by creating us with certain needs and desires such that we produce goods or offer services to meet the needs of others in exchange for their also meeting our needs (2 Thessalonians 3:6–12). We work, and through our work God provides. In this way work is like other vocations: God uses what we do in each vocation to provide for those whom we serve in that vocation. In our vocations we are, as Luther wrote, "masks of God."[13] Mothers and fathers provide God's care to their children; neighbors provide God's care to fellow neighbors through their friendliness, neighborhood watches, and acts of kindness; those who work provide God's care to all those who benefit from their labor, whether directly or indirectly. Said differently, work is one of several vocations God uses to promote human flourishing.[14]

12 See Luther's comments in the Large Catechism in the explanation of the Seventh Commandment (LC I 249) and the explanation of the Fourth Petition of the Lord's Prayer (LC III 74–75).

13 *Luther's Works* 14:114.

14 For a complementary understanding of vocation and human flourishing, see Michael Berg, *Vocation: The Setting for Human Flourishing* (Irvine, CA: New Reformation Publications/1517 Publishing, 2020), ch. 4.

The Work of Professionals

The work of professionals has its own unique features. Some professionals engage in work that has no direct beneficiary besides the company that pays them.[15] An accountant, for example, gathers financial information, summarizes it, and presents it to whichever management team needs it. The management team, however, is not the direct beneficiary of this work in the way that, say, I am the direct beneficiary of the work done by my physician. The management team itself derives only indirect benefits from the accountant's labor, whether in the form of satisfaction from proof that they did part of their job well over the past quarter or in the form of information that permits them to do the job for which they are being paid. Ultimately, it would seem, the beneficiary of the accountant's work is the firm—or perhaps the firm's owners. Yet if Luther is correct that God has called everyone to serve their neighbors by making us dependent upon one another within a network of need and labor, then the firm itself cannot continue to exist without providing benefits to people in exchange for the fruits of their labor, nor can it provide those benefits without providing other benefits (pay) to those who do the labor that generates the goods or services provided by the firm. In other words, the accountant helps to ensure that the firm has the knowledge of its financial activities necessary to continue providing goods and services to its customers and to continue paying its employees. Even if the accountant's reports have no clear direct beneficiary, the indirect beneficiaries of those reports include all of the firm's employees, suppliers, customers, partners, and so forth, as well as its owners. The same can be said for nearly anyone working in the firm. What might at first appear to be unimportant or insignificant work that does not help anyone turns out to have a great many indirect beneficiaries. God uses the accountant (or marketer or manager or team leader) to provide for other people in this world.

The situation is different for many members of the so-called professions. Lawyers, pastors, pharmacists, nurses, counselors, and other

15 See the introduction of this volume for definitions of the word "professional"; see Peter H. Nafzger's essay "Preaching to Professionals in a Secular World" in this volume for further discussion of the professions.

similar professionals typically have easily identifiable clients whom they serve. The specific structure of these professions creates unique ethical obligations for their members—they have well-defined ethical standards that are (hopefully) enforced by organizations composed of members of the profession, ethical standards that arise from the unique relationship between professional and client. The professional has technical knowledge, experience, and a certain amount of autonomy in the exercise of the duties of his or her job. Clients entrust sensitive information or their very bodies to the professional with the expectation that the professional will (1) use his or her knowledge and experience to assist the client in achieving certain goals, (2) safeguard the privacy and protect the confidentiality of the client, and (3) refrain from using what the client has revealed to enrich him- or herself or to compromise the client's well-being in any way. In exchange for the services and guarantees of the professional, the client pays a prearranged fee or rate.[16] Members of the professions make direct contributions to the flourishing of easily identifiable individuals. And as every member of these professions knows, these individuals have family members, employees or employers, neighbors, fellow community members, and so on. Thus, the work of members of the professions also has a large number of indirect beneficiaries. God uses members of the professions not merely to serve individual clients, but also to increase the flourishing of other people.

Conclusion

Professionals enjoy higher educational levels, greater social capital, and comparatively greater wealth than people in other occupations. They therefore have unique opportunities to hear and follow Christ's call to contribute to human flourishing in this world—and they have unique opportunities to work against Christ's call and cause great damage in the world. In an ideal world (a world without imperfect

16 This picture, of course, is idealized, as anyone working in the healthcare sector knows. Healthcare providers face constraints on their autonomy as healthcare managers and insurance companies seek to control costs. Similar forces are at work in other sectors. Yet members of the professions continue to maintain a sense that their first obligation is not to the organizations that employ them but to the clients they serve.

people) no one would ever knowingly promote his or her own interests at the expense of others, and the more powerful and more well-to-do would gladly shoulder the burdens unintentionally generated by the network of labor and need in which we live. Our world is, alas, not ideal, and neither moralistic preaching nor some perfect set of laws will ever make it ideal. It is inhabited by people who are imperfect. Some will act better, and some will act worse, but none will act perfectly. Christians seek forgiveness from Christ for acting imperfectly and they strive to show the same love to others that God has shown them in Christ as they await the day when Christ establishes "new heavens and a new earth in which righteousness dwells" (2 Peter 3:13).

In the meantime, the work of professionals is vitally important for maintaining the social fabric that makes the network of need and labor possible in its contemporary, complex form. Professionals must hold one another accountable for acting in ways that are consistent with ethical standards and that promote rather than detract from human flourishing. They must seek wise counsel about the effects that their decisions may have on their firms, their clients, the communities in which they operate, and the world at large. They must likewise provide wise counsel to and sometimes bring vocal pressure to bear on decision-makers within their firms, organizations, and communities as advocates for the people who will be affected by decisions. The call to preserve the social fabric and support human flourishing does not arise from a divine plan to reshape this world into a more godly order. It arises from the needs of real human beings in specific communities. It arises from the circumstances that cause them suffering or bring them joy, that keep them from thriving or help them to flourish. It is thus a call (a vocation) to serve our neighbors. And for Christians, it is a call (a vocation) to love others as Christ first loved us.

ECONOMIC SYSTEMS, VOCATION, AND HUMAN FLOURISHING FROM A LUTHERAN PERSPECTIVE

Van A. Mobley

Dr. Van A. Mobley is Professor of History and Economics at Concordia University Wisconsin, where he holds a dual appointment in the School of Arts and Sciences and the School of Business and Legal Studies. He worked in business, politics, and industry prior to coming to Concordia. He currently serves as the Village President for Thiensville, WI.

Martin Luther is best remembered for the key role he played in sparking the Protestant Reformation and thereby transforming the religious community of medieval Europe. Luther also provided keen insight into the changing economic conditions of his day and helped his contemporaries conceptualize their collective and individual economic activity in new and dynamic ways. By identifying the state (or government) as the institution responsible for regulating markets, by prioritizing labor as a component in the economic process, and by stressing the value of every market participant's occupation, Luther pointed toward an emerging type of economic system which was no longer feudal but not entirely capitalistic or communistic either. While Luther never devised a name for the economic system he favored, perhaps it is best described as a "mixed system." Since Luther's day the most successful nations have had a mixed system, and those that have adopted radically capitalistic or communistic systems have floundered. It's no wonder, then, that Luther is often identified as one of the most influential thinkers of the modern age.

Luther's economic ideas emerged in the sixteenth-century Holy Roman Empire (much of which was later incorporated into the modern state of Germany), but that does not mean they are outmoded in our postmodern world. Considering them carefully provides insight into the nature of our own economic predicament and generates helpful theoretical and practical insights. Luther never imagined he could prescribe the perfect way to organize a mixed system any more than he could spell out precisely what persons could or should do as they selected an occupation and pursued it. Luther expected perfection to reign among us humans only once Christ returns and transforms us along with the fallen world our sin had generated, and he was suspicious of anyone who suggested otherwise. His blunt, realistic, devout temperament shaped his perspective on our individual and collective economic prospects, and it inoculated him and his followers from the more utopian snares that have subsequently mesmerized radical capitalistic and communistic thinkers, as well as their devotees.

Besides rejecting perfection as a suitable expectation for either individual or collective economic effort, Luther also rebuffed the idea that perfection is generated by some impersonal socioeconomic process. For example, he did not think participation in market activities would necessarily improve a person's moral character. Indeed, participating in the market is just as likely to generate sinners as saints. From Luther's perspective, there is room for variety, experimentation, and improvement in our economic endeavors, and human flourishing in an economic sense depends upon the progress such activity can produce. But at best, economic flourishing can bring only provisional gratification, and it must be conducted within certain boundaries and with limited expectations. When humans cross the line, as it were (either individually or collectively) such violations generate economic and moral regress rather than progress. Step back far enough from the rush of time, his writings suggest, and one notices that the arc of history doesn't trend up or down—it fluctuates. "Remember where the lines are, and your limitations. Work hard in the occupation to which you are called, and wait upon the Lord," Luther seems to be telling us across the centuries. Figuring out where the economic and ethical lines are, or should be, and staying within them, while at the same time laboring within an occupation and waiting on the Lord, has never been an easy task, and it seems to be getting harder. Thank goodness we can draw upon Luther's insights as we seek to chart fresh paths forward in a rapidly changing world!

Economic Systems and Luther's Thought

The potentially different economic systems that might be or have been adopted since Luther's time are often conceptualized in terms of a spectrum. "Extreme capitalism" is on one end of the spectrum. All the resources in such a system are owned by private individuals who are also market participants within it, and the market participants organize the resources under their control and interact with one another free from government supervision or protection, with an eye toward maximizing their own profits. "Extreme communism" is on the other end of the spectrum. All the resources in this system are directed and controlled by a powerful, and perhaps totalitarian, central government. Whether it consists of one or several decision-makers, this central government views the people and materials inside its boundaries as resources to be directed, organized, and distributed (with force if necessary) in pursuit of whatever objective or objectives the central authority identifies. Scattered between extreme capitalism on one end of the spectrum and extreme communism on the other end are a seemingly infinite variety of mixed economic systems. Such mixed systems contain some areas in which a governing authority uses persuasion if possible and force if necessary to direct resources toward certain objectives and/or toward protecting certain boundaries, such as property rights. It also contains other areas where market participants have autonomy to direct themselves and the resources they command however they please. Luther preferred the mixed systems in the middle and denounced the poles as radical extremes.

It is possible to spend a lifetime comparing and contrasting the advantages and disadvantages of the infinite variety of economic systems along the spectrum identified above. For example, in relation to its private sector, Sweden's government is much larger than is the US government in relation to its private sector, but both the United States and Sweden still have mixed economies and mixed systems. The US system simply falls more toward the capitalism side of the spectrum than does the Swedish one. Furthermore, because many of the world's mixed systems have been mixed together in different ways over the years (and/or are constantly being remixed, thereby causing them to oscillate one way or the other along the spectrum), it is possible to amass and subsequently compare and contrast data indicating how the competing mixes stack up against one another. Which mix is more efficient or less efficient, more just or less just, more innovative or less innovative, more growth oriented or less growth oriented, more environmentally friendly or less environmentally friendly, more aesthetically pleasing or less aesthetically pleasing, more stable or less stable, and so on? There is a dense economic forest to explore for those who want to ask and answer such questions. Luther declined to spend much time exploring the economic forest, not because he thought doing so was uninteresting or unimportant but rather, it seems, because he felt no call to delve too deeply into the intricacies of economic theory and practice. It was not his vocation. He was a pastor, not an economist. But Luther knew enough to reject the extreme capitalistic and extreme communistic options at the opposing ends of the spectrum and to provide clear advice concerning habits and proclivities that should be cultivated and avoided to help maintain a position between the two poles and thereby prevent oneself and the system of which one is a part from lurching too close to one or the other of the extremes. Luther also gave numerous examples concerning how decision-makers should pick and choose among the mixed systems as well as other examples describing how individuals operating within such mixed systems should behave.

Before jumping to some of the examples Luther provided to illustrate how he thought government decision-makers and market participants should navigate the mixed system he hoped they would adopt, it is necessary to say a bit more about the theological considerations that prompted Luther to reject both extreme capitalism and extreme communism. Luther believed the nature and consequences of human sin made any prosperous, happy, and productive human individual or social grouping inherently fragile. Luther thought that, when left to their own unchecked devices, human beings within any system (no matter what role or vocation they played within it) tended to replace legitimate, appropriate objectives with inappropriate ones, even though it was easy to anticipate that the pursuit of such inappropriate objectives would ruin their own lives, destroy the lives of those around them, and wreck the systems of which they were a part.[1] Left to their own devices, human beings generate crises, not harmonious flourishing. Hence we pray that the Lord grant us His peace.

While Luther lived before the modern world's most influential and persuasive capitalistic and communistic thinkers emerged, he would have rejected the premises of some of their central arguments. For example, he thought seeking to maximize one's private economic profit in any given circumstance was sinful. Luther would not countenance such an objective even if some procapitalistic economist suggested that in time market forces could or would harmonize and tame self-interested economic actors seeking to maximize their own profit and produce an idyllic sort of spontaneous order. "No," we can hear Luther pronouncing boldly. It is salutary to earn a *legitimate* profit while pursuing one's occupation. But allowing the desire to *maximize* one's own profit to shape one's economic decision-making is sinful, and it will result in a downward spiral both for the person who makes that decision as well as for his or her community, no matter what some modern economist might suggest.[2] After all, "the love of money is a root of all kinds of evils" (1 Timothy 6:10). Focusing on profit maximization prevents us from hearing the Lord's call.

Likewise, Luther would reject the idea that by exalting a single individual or small group of individuals into a powerful central government that controlled all aspects of a particular economic system, and having that person or group conceptualize and execute planning for the entire system from the center outward, it would be possible to transform the boundaries of earthly existence and create a workers' paradise.[3] "You and your revolutionary experts are so puffed with pride," we can almost hear Luther scolding Lenin if he had been alive on the eve of the Communist Revolution, "that in the pursuit of your self-projected vision of a 'workers' paradise' you will produce a hell on earth."

1 See, for example, "Trade and Usury," *Luther's Works* 45:246–49.

2 See, for example, Luther's explanation of the Seventh Commandment in the Large Catechism.

3 Luther suggested that the temporal authorities might appoint "wise and honest men" to set prices for certain commodities, but he also pointed out that fair prices can never be governed either by writing or speaking (*Luther's Works* 25:249). And of course, Luther believed that Christians, who might act wisely and honestly, are quite rare (*Luther's Works* 25:258).

It is better, Luther indicated, to be content with imperfect, mixed systems that check our capitalistic or communistic enthusiasms, and allow God's call to be heard and answered rather than to embrace reckless schemes rooted in the love of money or pride.

Luther linked the mixed system for which he advocated to the vocation of the participants within it and the command God gave humans to labor inside the occupation to which they have been called. He saw value in any occupation to which people had been called, and he thought people should enter into these occupations, not because they were in pursuit of riches or had been directed to do so by government but rather in response to God's call to serve their neighbors. The Almighty is active in the world, and we are all better off when we learn to hear and respond to His call. Luther didn't expect the mixed systems he preferred to create heaven on earth, but he did think they were more likely to generate human flourishing than either of the systems on the far edges of the spectrum.

Luther lived at the beginning of the modern age, not the end, so he had no opportunity to examine the systems designed by the most sophisticated capitalist and communist ideologues or the historical record of those nations where attempts were made to implement such systems. But Luther espied the flaws at the foundation of the pure capitalist and communist systems and anticipated their outcomes. He offered practical advice to help orient his audience toward the mixed, muddled, imperfect space where mixed systems are located and occupations are pursued, as well as practical advice concerning how individuals and systems could avoid creating or succumbing to situations that would drive them to extremes. Upon reflection, it is evident that Luther's recipe for success in an occupation still resonates in today's world.

Luther on Monopolies and the Emergence of Extreme Capitalism

One of the flaws Luther noticed in the emerging mixed economy of his day was monopolies. His analysis of their causes and impacts tells us much about his understanding of the economic processes that were reshaping the European economy during his era, and it differentiates him from later, more capitalistic thinkers whose works have shaped modern economics textbooks. On some issues, however, Luther and the modern economists align. For example, Luther and the modern textbook economists agree that during the medieval period most Europeans lived on relatively self-sufficient manors. Most markets were local, and transactions were often via barter. Individuals were either largely self-sufficient or they worked to create goods and services they traded for goods and services generated by other people in their locality. There was little scope for the rise of extraordinarily rich people and/or corporations spanning large areas. There was little need or ability to amass large sums of money. The nature of the economic environment itself limited the scope of economic ambition.

The stable, relatively self-sufficient manorial economy that characterized much of the Holy Roman Empire during the medieval period began to change shortly before Luther's birth, and the change accelerated throughout his life. The old, primarily barter economy was replaced with a money economy, and the amount of money within the system began to grow and grow while circulating at a faster and faster pace. Increasingly large economic organizations appeared. Instead of doing their business within a single manor or principality or even within the Holy Roman Empire, globalizing organizations emerged that spanned the entire Empire and beyond. As they did so, the ambitions of some of the market participants began to mushroom as well.

As the old barter economy faded and the more modern money economy emerged, market participants found it possible to work for profit rather than to create a concrete object or service available for consumption or barter within a local community. Modern textbook economists have devised models which demonstrate that in such a context, profits are maximized by those persons who stumble upon or create a monopoly for themselves in the production and/or distribution of a particular good or service. Once a monopoly is formed (for example, via legislative or legal action, by driving other producers out of business, by accident, etc.), the monopolist labors less on, makes fewer of, and charges more for the goods and services he or she provides than would be the case if he or she inhabited a competitive market. Economic models found in today's textbooks explain that monopolists *act* differently than persons who participate in regular old competitive markets. Whereas the monopolist constrains supply and sets prices, producers in a competitive market accept the price generated outside themselves by the market and produce more than a monopolist. But the economic textbooks *assume* persons who participate in competitive markets have the same *motives* as the monopolist. According to the textbooks, all economic actors *seek* to maximize their own profits. The difference between a monopolist and a normal market participant in a competitive or mixed system isn't the *motive* that propels the two different types of participants (they are both profit maximizers); it is the particular *circumstances* he or she faces (i.e., one has the ability to constrain supply, set prices, and be a profit-maximizing monopolist, while the other must accept market prices and does not have an opportunity to maximize profits as a monopolist).

Luther rejected the way modern textbook economists conceptualize the appropriate motivations and objectives of market participants before the textbook economists even made their conceptualizations! Luther didn't think monopolistic behavior sprang up when particular circumstances within a market system emerged; he thought it emerged from unchecked sinful desires within some market participants, who then created or took advantage of circumstances that allowed them to create monopolies, behave like monopolists, and maximize their own profits. Furthermore, Luther thought that if this sin (i.e., the maximizing of one's own profit by creating a monopoly or taking advantage of a circumstance that allowed one to enjoy monopolistic profits) were left unchecked and became widespread, it would wreck the mixed system he preferred and diminish the human flourishing which the broadening of horizons generated by the discoveries of the early modern age allowed him to contemplate.[4] Instead of seeking to master their occupation and becoming better at it (i.e., making more, better goods and services to suit the needs of one's neighbors with the resources one commanded),

4 See *Luther's Works* 45:261–63.

each market participant would seek to acquire a monopoly, constrain the supply of the good or service they provided, work less and produce less than would otherwise be the case, and charge more for it, thereby maximizing the monopolists' own profit. If the future belonged to the profit-maximizing monopolists, Luther didn't see economic flourishing in the future. Instead, he saw economic crisis and decline.

Luther called on the people of his day to nip the monopolistic spirit in the bud—and if an individual could not or would not control his or her own propensity to sin in this regard, Luther called on the government to check the sin via regulation and law. From Luther's perspective, it is sinful for a Christian who is practicing an occupation to make maximizing profit the primary objective as did the monopolist, even if his or her occupation provided opportunities to do so. He denounced monopolists as the "greedy ones" who "are not worthy to be called human beings or to live among men; they are not even worth admonishing or instructing."[5] Instead, Luther called upon the government to crush the monopolists. He proclaimed, "The temporal authorities would do right if they took from such fellows everything they had, and drove them out of the country."[6] Clearly, Luther disliked monopolists. He said harsh things about them, and this ought not be whitewashed or overlooked.

Monopolies, Extreme Communism, and the Drive for a "Workers' Paradise"

In the United States, everyone pretty much agrees with Luther that monopolies do and will emerge within the context of our mixed system, and that when they do they should be broken up or regulated or they will destroy the mixed system we enjoy. Where disagreement emerges in our mixed system is over the process by which monopolies are identified and the identity of the persons or organizations that should be classified as monopolists at any given time. In other nations at other times, there have been different perspectives on the role of the monopolist. For example, in the late nineteenth and early twentieth centuries, at roughly the same moment in historical time when

5 *Luther's Works* 45:264–65.

6 *Luther's Works* 45:265.

President Theodore Roosevelt was identifying and busting up monopolies within the American mixed system, Vladimir Lenin, one of history's foremost communists, also noticed the mixed systems of Europe were spawning profit-maximizing monopolists and monopolies. But whereas Roosevelt was inclined to annihilate or regulate monopolies in order to prevent them from destroying the mixed system within which they had emerged, Lenin argued that the emergence of monopolies within the world's mixed systems would eventually pave the way for the triumph of communism, the type of economic system he preferred. So from Lenin's perspective, monopolists should be tolerated, and perhaps even encouraged, at least for a while. How is it that a communist like Lenin could be so favorably inclined (at least momentarily) toward profit-maximizing capitalists like the monopolists?

To understand why, it is helpful to recall the spectrum of possible economic systems we sketched earlier. On one end of the spectrum we have extreme capitalism, dominated by those who are motivated by the desire to maximize their own profit. On the other end we have the communist system, characterized by a powerful central government that directs all the persons in the system toward ends it determines regardless of the individual objectives or motivations of the persons who inhabit the system. Between these two extreme poles are all the varieties of mixed systems, where people are free to direct themselves in some areas but not others, and where the motivations that propel individuals are multitudinous and hence opaque. Lenin thought it would be difficult, and maybe impossible, to persuade human beings to move from a mixed system, within which they had at least some autonomy, to a communist system, where none but the one or very few at the center of the government had any autonomy at all. But Lenin thought it was undeniable that, in his time, humans *were moving* from mixed systems in the middle of the spectrum toward the pole of extreme capitalism dominated by profit-maximizing monopolists. He also noticed that while the monopolists were amassing huge profits for themselves, they were steadily impoverishing the other inhabitants of the mixed system and growing to such an immense size that they threatened to overtake the governments of the mixed system in terms of power and influence. From Lenin's perspective, this was creating a crisis that would overwhelm the mixed systems. Thus, Lenin thought the movement toward the pole of extreme capitalism would end up (paradoxically enough) creating conditions within which extreme communism would triumph.

Lenin used this conceptual understanding of the economic circumstances emerging about him to help himself, and the Bolshevik Party he led, seize power in Russia in 1917 and begin a century-long project to reorganize that immense country along communistic lines. We must remember that from Lenin's perspective the communist revolution was made possible, at least in part, by the appearance and spread of the profit-maximizing monopolists, who drove the mixed system within which they emerged and of which they were a part toward the extremely capitalistic pole. But whereas Luther denounced the sin of the self-absorbed profit-maximizing monopolists, those "greedy ones" who drove things toward a crisis, Lenin thought the "greedy ones" were "useful idiots" who paved the way for the emergence of the Communists.

Avoiding the Extremes and Working in a Vocation

One of the great ironies of Lenin's career is that shortly after the Communist revolutionaries seized power in Russia and launched their attempt to transform the system there into a communist system, he noticed something he had failed to anticipate but which would have been no surprise to Martin Luther. The Communist-led movement away from the extreme capitalist pole and toward the extreme communistic pole proved incapable of resolving the crisis in Russia. Instead, under Lenin's government Russia jumped away from the frying pan of extreme capitalism and into the fire of extreme communism. Things did not get better—they kept getting worse. Faced with this unexpected shock, Lenin cracked. He changed course and headed back toward a mixed system of the sort that had prevailed prior to the emergence of the crisis the Communists had originally exploited to gain power and then exacerbated once they had gained power. The New Economic Policy (NEP), which was implemented in the USSR during the 1920s, was designed to create (and actually did create) a mixed system that allowed individuals to own private property, exercise their own autonomy, and seek profits—albeit a mixed system located pretty far toward the communist pole of the spectrum.

In light of Lenin's change in direction, it is easy to imagine Luther congratulating him and asking him, since Lenin was now the ruler of Russia, "Why not stop lurching back and forth between the radical poles and instead forge a congenial mixed system where you can settle in, be still, and let the inhabitants of Russia listen carefully to the Lord's call and respond to it by pursuing their occupation as a vocation? If your government, whatever you want to call it, manages to hold such a middle position, the people you govern will certainly flourish more than is likely if they inhabit a system located too far toward one or the other of the poles." To which we can imagine a frustrated Lenin tossing up his hands and replying, "How, exactly, do you expect us to stop the lurching? How do we avoid overshooting now that we have left the extreme communism pole and headed back for the middle?"

Luther's response to such an inquiry would probably have been twofold. First, Luther would probably have advised the inhabitants of the USSR during the period of the NEP to focus on the occupations they were now free to pursue as a result of the Soviet government's new policy. And if an individual Russian felt him- or herself called to pursue an occupation in one of the competitive market areas now made available by the NEP, they would have to sell their product. This call, Luther expected, would generate some interesting questions in the heads of the market participants, questions like,

> "How dear may I sell? How am I to arrive at what is fair and right so I do not take increase from neighbor or overcharge him?" Answer: That is something that will never be governed either by writing or speaking. . . . In this respect, therefore, everything is and must remain uncertain. . . . Where the price of goods is not fixed either by

> law or custom, and you must fix it yourself, here one can truly give you no instructions but only lay it on your conscience to be careful not to overcharge your neighbor, and to seek a modest living, not the goals of greed. . . . Therefore, you must make up your mind to seek in your trading only an adequate living.[7]

Here we see Luther proposing as a goal for the capitalist not profit maximization but rather an "adequate living." From Luther's perspective, a mixed system containing capitalists who sought an "adequate living" rather than profit maximization would be fine.

The second part of Luther's answer would be aimed not at the market participants who live under a government but instead at the person or persons who run the government. From Luther's perspective, it was all about striking a governmental balance. The arm of government should not extend too much or too little.

> For where it [government] is given too wide a scope, intolerable and terrible injury follows; on the other hand, injury is also inevitable where it is restricted too narrowly. In the former case, the temporal authority punishes too much; in the latter case, it punishes too little. To err in this direction, however, and punish too little is more tolerable, for it is always better to let a scoundrel live than to put a godly man to death. The world has plenty of scoundrels anyway and must continue to have them, but godly men are scarce.[8]

Conclusion

From Luther's perspective, mixed systems which contain a limited government that avoids trying to do too much and allows the persons

7 *Luther's Works* 45:249–50.

8 *Luther's Works* 45:104–5.

who inhabit them to procure an adequate living while pursuing the occupation to which they have been called represent the best sort of economic system we can attain in our fallen world. Creating such systems is hard, and once created they are vulnerable to decay. For instance, as we have seen, the nongovernmental participants in a mixed system can undermine it by becoming too greedy and driving it toward the pole of extreme capitalism or by ceasing to work and thereby giving it no energy or momentum. On the other hand, the government can undermine it by seeking to control too much and thereby driving it to the pole of extreme communism, or by neglecting to govern enough and allowing the growth of destructive forces like monopolies. From Luther's perspective, when mixed systems do emerge, they foster human flourishing far more than do systems on the extremes. He called Christians to respond to God's call and pursue their vocations, maintain the appropriate balance in them, and pray that they will be blessed. For while we can respond to God's call, ultimately the creation and maintenance of our world is the result of His work, which is why we trust in Him for our ultimate salvation and pray that He will bless us in our fallen world.

Further Reading

Max Weber's *The Protestant Ethic and the Spirit of Capitalism* helped spark a tremendous debate over the origins of capitalism in the modern world and the role the Protestant Reformation played in shaping its origins and rise. In Weber's construction of the narrative, Protestantism spawned capitalism and fueled its rise, but Luther, the greatest of the Protestant reformers, was not himself particularly capitalistic. Later scholars, such as R. H. Tawney in *Religion and the Rise of Capitalism*, have fleshed out Weber's narrative, and by doing so granted Luther none of the blame or credit for the rise of capitalism. In Tawney's reading of the story, Luther was a backward-looking rather than a forward-looking thinker, at least when it came to economic topics. More recent scholars such as Philipp Robinson Rössner in *Freedom and Capitalism in Early Modern Europe: Mercantilism and the Making of the Modern Economic Mind* (Palgrave Macmillan, 2020) have pointed out that several varieties of capitalism have emerged in the period since Luther's day and that Luther's thought helped shape, and is congenial toward, some, if not all, of these varieties of capitalism. My own view is that Luther's economic thought has an honorable place in a long line of economic theorists who, like Adam Smith, argue that human flourishing is most vibrant when individuals have the freedom to serve one another by pursuing their occupations as vocations in free market systems, with an eye toward making adequate, rather than maximum, profits. Neither Adam Smith nor Martin Luther would ever cavil about the old capitalist adage that the wise capitalist "leaves a little something on the table" for his trading partners.

PREACHING TO PROFESSIONALS IN A SECULAR WORLD

Peter H. Nafzger

Rev. Peter H. Nafzger, PhD, is Associate Professor of Practical Theology and Director of Student Life at Concordia Seminary, St. Louis. He teaches courses in homiletics, pastoral ministry, and systematic theology. Prior to coming to Concordia Seminary, he served as the pastor of New Life Church—Lutheran in Hugo, MN, and guest professor at Concordia University, St. Paul, MN.

This book is aimed at members of the professions. It tries to help them imagine their work as vocational service through which God works toward the broader goal of human flourishing. This chapter has a different audience. It is written to those whose vocation is to speak. Through their speaking, they aim to shape the lives of the professionals (and others) for good. In other words, this chapter is for preachers.

The Vocation of Preacher

Christian preachers occupy an ambitious vocation. Martin Luther King Jr. described it as a "vocation of agony."[1] Preachers are called to speak the truth about God, the universe, and the human condition. Even more, they are called to speak *for* God by proclaiming His commands and promises. But faithful preaching demands more than confidence in Jesus and the courage to go public. It also calls for endurance to do the necessary work of preparation each week and a lifelong willingness to listen to those who they hope will listen to them. To speak a word on target, they must study the context of their hearers as closely

1 Martin Luther King Jr., "Beyond Vietnam: A Time to Break Silence" (speech delivered April 4, 1967, at Riverside Church, New York City); Richard Lischer quotes this in *The End of Words: The Language of Reconciliation in a Culture of Violence* (Grand Rapids, MI: Eerdmans, 2005), 20. Lischer also quotes Martin Luther, "I would rather be stretched upon a wheel or carry stones than preach one sermon" (*Luther's Works* 51:222). One of my homiletics professors, Rev. Francis Rossow, described preaching as both "an agony and an ecstasy." He promised my classmates and I would experience both. He was right.

as they study the Scriptures.[2] Fred Craddock names the stakes: "Taking the congregation out of context is as much a violation of the Word of God as taking the scripture out of context. . . . The one who preaches the same regardless of who comes to hear would probably preach the same regardless of whether anyone came to hear, and the preacher may very well soon have that opportunity."[3]

Understanding the world of the hearers enables preachers to speak directly into their lives. But preachers do more than *inform* their hearers. They also *form* their hearers and their conception of the world around them. Through diligent study of both the world of the Scriptures and the world of the hearers, preachers uncover ways in which the hearers' world is at odds with the biblical world. Then, by proclaiming the commands and promises of Christ, the preacher remakes their world through words.[4]

The Secular World of the Twenty-First-Century Professional

Every once in a while we come across someone behaving strangely and we think to ourselves that he is living in his own little world. It is true. He is. But so are all of us. Depending in large part on the vocations we occupy, each of us lives in our own version of the world. Sometimes we share this world with others because of a common vocation. Members of the legal professions, for example, live in a world shaped by motions and briefs, jury selections and sentence hearings, defendants, witnesses, and legal opinions. College coaches, in contrast, live in a world shaped by wins and losses, press conferences and player egos, recruitment trips, eligibility requirements, and alumni relations. To participate in a profession is to exist in a specific world with its own language, its own challenges, and its own goals. But it is also true

2 David R. Schmitt calls this part of the preaching task "hearer interpretation" and notes that it requires careful attention in every sermon. See "The Tapestry of Preaching," *Concordia Journal* 37, no. 2 (Spring 2011): 107–29.

3 Fred Craddock, *As One Without Authority*, 4th ed. (St. Louis, MO: Chalice Press, 2001), 104.

4 For more about preaching as remaking worlds, see Peter H. Nafzger, "The Preacher as Worldmaker: Reflections of the Nature and Purpose of Christian Preaching" *Concordia Journal* 45, no. 1 (Winter 2019): 51–61.

that professionals live in a broader "professional world" that shares a number of fundamental characteristics. The contours of that world are the subject of this chapter.

What is the world of the twenty-first-century professional? In *A Secular Age*, Charles Taylor explores a fundamental transformation that has taken place in the Western world over the last five hundred years.[5] It has to do with religious belief and its role in our collective social imagination. To summarize a long and complex story, at the beginning of the sixteenth century it was virtually impossible *not* to believe in God. Everyone believed that God created all things, that history was progressing toward a final day of judgment, and that the Scriptures were divine and uniquely authoritative. These beliefs formed the unquestioned backdrop for life and work. But that is no longer the case. For many today, and for Western society as a whole, disbelief in God is not only easy but inescapable. The idea that God created all things is no longer considered scientifically plausible, warnings of a future day of judgment are dismissed as rantings of wild-eyed street prophets, and the Bible is approached as a literary and cultural artifact rather than the Word of God.[6]

This transformation, argues Taylor, coincides with and contributes to the rise of what he calls "exclusive humanism."[7] Humanism is belief in the value, goodness, and potential of humanity. It emphasizes dignity, freedom, and progress of the human species. Humanism has taken many forms over the centuries, including a Christian form during the Reformation. But the version Taylor has in mind is "exclusive." That is, it imagines human existence as self-sufficient, both in terms of origins and ends. It insists that human existence has no transcendent standard or guide, no externally determined goal or function. Rather than finding their place within an ordered universe fashioned by an almighty Creator, humans are responsible for constructing their own place and establishing their own order. If they are to flourish, it is up to them to

5 Charles Taylor, *A Secular Age* (Cambridge, MA: Harvard University Press, 2007).

6 This is not to say that some people do not believe these things. But now they must be explicitly justified and defended.

7 Taylor, *A Secular Age*, 19.

determine what counts as flourishing as well as to develop the means by which this flourishing takes place. In other words, we are on our own.

Taylor's diagnosis of our current situation has far-reaching implications for every vocation. But when thinking specifically about professionals and the world in which they live, three common characteristics stand out as foundational for a preacher to recognize. Their world is shaped by (1) a formalized system of education, (2) a definite sense of ethical accountability, and (3) an interminable quest for personal security.

A Formalized System of Education

Participation in the professions in the twenty-first century is safely guarded by a formalized system of education. Accredited degrees, specialized licenses, renewable certifications, and continuing education requirements keep the system humming. As each professional field grows in its collective knowledge and skill, the system becomes even more deeply entrenched and increasingly specialized. Several results have followed. First, the specialized nature of each field has made professional practice virtually impossible without participation in the system. Home remedies and do-it-yourself tutorials work for minor matters. But when taxes get complicated and reading glasses no longer cut it, you need help from a professional. Second, the extent of the educational requirements has created a two-tiered society. Corresponding to the class of professionals is a much larger class of lay people who depend on them. As a result, the professional finds herself in an increasingly elevated position of authority. Third, and most significant for preachers, the training received by most professionals in this system lacks an explicit religious commitment. The religious faith of those who participate in this system is not necessarily rejected or prohibited. But, like religion in general in a secular age, it is often relegated to the realm of the private.

This formalized educational system is a gift from God. Without a doubt, it has raised the standards of credentialed practice and contributed to human flourishing in ways that would have been unimaginable in previous generations. But it also presents challenges—both for Christian professionals and those who preach to them. For professionals, their specialized training is usually disconnected from their religious beliefs, which means they are not trained to recognize their work as participation in the God's work in this world. This is because the narrative context in which their training has taken place does not match the Christian account of the world. Christians, for example, live according to a specific narrative that begins with a Creator who made all things and to whom all people are accountable. In this narrative, every human life has dignity and value because it has been made by God. This story will come to an end when all people—both the living and the dead—stand before God on a day of final judgment.

These narrative foundations help Christians (professionals and otherwise) answer larger metaphysical questions about the origins, standards, and ends of human life and work. When this narrative context is lacking—as it is in the formalized system of education expected of professions—so also is the Christian professionals' ability to imagine themselves and their work rightly. Complicating matters is the fact that, when the formalized system of educational training *does* offer answers, they are not always compatible with a Christian conception of the world. As a result, the professionals' education does not equip them to imagine their work rightly as part of the Christian narrative.

A Sense of Ethical Responsibility

As a field of study, ethics is concerned with developing and conforming to a set of rules and expectations by which people are expected to live. It deals with right conduct. Members of the professions are highly conscious of the ethical standards that govern their work. Entrance into and continued participation in the profession usually depends on compliance with a detailed code of ethics that has been developed by peers within the same profession and is, in theory, rigorously enforced. Violation of the code results in disciplinary action and potential exclusion from the profession.

This ethical code is primarily one-sided. That is, professionals have ethical obligations to their clients that are not reciprocal. This is because of *access*. While specifics vary across professions, those who seek service from professionals grant them access to sensitive parts of their lives. Someone seeking therapy offers the professional counselor access to his past (and present) feelings, thoughts, and behavior; someone seeking medical care offers the nurse access to her body; someone seeking financial service offers an accountant access to his finances and property. Clients entrust the professional with intimate access, expecting that the professional will maintain a strict level of confidentiality and use this access for their good.

The ethical accountability required of professionals contributes significantly to human flourishing. Without the fiduciary trust it supports, normal people would lack confidence to benefit from the service of professionals. At the same time, the sense of ethical accountability in a secular world presents two related challenges for Christian professionals. First, the ethical standards that govern each profession are culturally determined. For example, the *Model Rules of Professional Conduct* of the American Bar Association states, "A lawyer's conduct should conform to the requirements of the law."[8] This provides stability to the ethical code. But this stability lasts only as long as laws remain constant. When legislation changes, the standard for professional conduct also changes. What counts as ethical behavior in one generation may not in another. This raises questions, not only about specific ethical rules but about the stability of *any* ethical standard.

This leads to a second, more foundationally significant challenge. In a secular age, the end or *telos* of ethical behavior is lacking. The question "Why?" has no satisfactory answer. Why should someone treat others ethically? Why should a surgeon do no harm? Why should a lawyer engage in pro bono work? Why should a teacher spend time outside of class with the struggling student? In a secular age, appeal to God for answers to such questions is off the table. Humans are left to their own good will, which, as it turns out, is not as good as we would like to think.[9]

8 American Bar Association, *Model Rules of Professional Conduct*, Preamble, 5, https://www.americanbar.org/groups/professional_responsibility/publications/model_rules_of_professional_conduct/model_rules_of_professional_conduct_preamble_scope/ (accessed July 15, 2022).

9 So Alasdair MacIntyre likens our current moral situation to the dark ages. See *After Virtue*, 3rd ed. (Notre Dame, IN: Notre Dame University Press, 2007), 263.

A Search for Personal Security

Many reasons motivate a person to pursue a professional vocation. Some desire to use their particular set of skills and interests. Some follow the familiar lead of a parent or friend. Some seek to make a meaningful impact on the world. Among these reasons is the promise that professional careers offer personal security.

When thinking about "personal security," both words are important. Professionals, like all people, are constantly looking for personal *security*. They long for a source of stability to help them endure the uncertainties in life caused by danger, disappointment, and death. The professions seem to offer more than other vocations. Perhaps most obviously, the relatively high compensation that accompanies many professions promises financial security.[10] This, in turn, supports other forms of security. With higher compensation comes higher quality health care, safer homes and neighborhoods, and more time for leisure and vacation. The professions also promise a type of security that comes through status. Graduates of prestigious educational institutions are treated with high levels of respect. So are many professionals. Medical and educational professionals, for example, are among the most respected occupations in the country.[11] The security found in what other people think of one's work is only part of the story, however. Many professionals find their identity in what they do for a living. Serving in a vocation that is perceived to be good for society helps you sleep well at night, believing that what you do for a living helps make the world a better place.

The security sought by professionals is also *personal* security. Professionals (like most people) are focused especially on establishing security for themselves (and perhaps also for their immediate families).

10 According to the US Bureau of Labor Statistics, seventeen of the top twenty highest-paying jobs in 2023 are in the professions; most of them are in the medical field ("Occupational Outlook Handbook," https://www.bls.gov/ooh/highest-paying.htm, accessed October 21, 2023). This is not lost on college admissions departments, many of which post the starting salary for their preprofessional programs. See, for example, the "Career Outcomes" section of Concordia University Nebraska's information page for the prepharmacy undergraduate degree (https://cune.edu/academics/undergraduate/pre-pharmacy; accessed October 21, 2023).

11 Lydia Saad, "Military Brass, Judges Among Professions at New Image Lows," January 12, 2022, https://news.gallup.com/poll/388649/military-brass-judges-among-professions-new-image-lows.aspx.

To achieve this personal security, professionals are willing to make significant personal sacrifices. These include financial sacrifices to afford the necessary education, relational sacrifices that come with the postponement of marriage and children, and time sacrifices that come from a willingness to work long hours toward advancement. Overwork and busyness are common among professionals in a secular age.[12]

There are at least two significant challenges to this search for personal security. First, the conception of personal *security* is fragile. Second, the focus on *personal* security often leaves aside concern for the neighbor.

The World (Re)Made through Preaching

As preachers study the world of professionals, they find much to affirm. The system of education serves to advance human knowledge and skill, thereby enabling each profession to contribute more fully to human flourishing. The sense of ethical accountability holds professionals to a high standard of behavior, thereby instilling confidence in clients who seek their help. The search for personal security motivates professionals to excel in their field, thereby equipping them to provide increasingly beneficial service to others. At the same time, the secular nature of the professional world creates challenges for Christians. These challenge offer direction for how preachers should address the professionals in their congregations.

Education Properly Located

In Acts 17, Paul visited Athens. There he encountered people who spent their time discussing the latest teachings and philosophies—not unlike those who occupy present-day institutions of higher learning. Eventually he would stand up to deliver a famous sermon at the Areopagus. But before opening his mouth to preach, he spent time

12 Professionals are notorious for failing to take their allotted vacation time and for bringing work with them when they do take a vacation. The irony is that they are more able to afford vacation (both in terms of time and money) than many other occupations. David Zahl describes the "seculosity" of busyness and work as two means of self-justification. See *Seculosity: How Career, Parenting, Technology, Food, Politics, and Romance Became Our New Religion and What to Do about It* (Minneapolis: Fortress Press, 2019).

listening to those who would listen to him. He visited their marketplaces. He spoke with their philosophers. He observed their worship. He noticed that they worshiped a host of false gods, including one that remained unknown. There was much he would need to confront. But he also found something to affirm. Their poets were not far off. The altar to the unknown god was more incomplete than wrong. They had part of the story right but not the whole. As Paul began his sermon, he affirmed their religious inclinations. From there he proceeded to fill in the narrative gaps. He made known their unknown object of worship by identifying the one true God as the Creator of all things. This God is intimately involved in the lives of all His human creatures, providing daily breath and boundaries for all human life. More than that, this God desires that all human creatures would seek a relationship with Him. To that end, Paul said, God calls all people to repent and return to Him before the day of judgment. The vindication of these claims, and the one on whom the entire story depends, is the man God raised from the dead, namely, Jesus.

Paul's approach to preaching in Athens provides guidance for those who are called to preach to professionals in a secular world. Like the people in Athens, professionals have been trained in an educational system whose underlying narrative is disconnected from the biblical narrative. The preacher's job is to identify these differences and proclaim the fullness of the biblical story that provides the context for all life and work. This story begins at creation and ends with the new creation. It is driven by God's plan to restore what was lost when humankind fell into sin and death. At the center is Jesus, through whom and for whom all things were made, and who holds all things together. He is the promised Messiah and Son of God who came to redeem God's chosen people. They rejected Him, however, and put Him to death on a cross. But He did not stay dead. On the third day He rose again. His resurrection justified His claims and vindicated Him as the Lord over all things. After rising, He sent His followers to continue His mission of calling all people everywhere to repent and believe His promises of forgiveness, life, and salvation. He ascended into heaven with the promise to come again on the Last Day to finish what He started and make all things new. In the meantime, His people continue His work through loving service toward one another and all people.[13]

Within this larger story, preachers can affirm much of what professionals have learned and developed in their formalized system of education. All true knowledge is knowledge of the Creator and His creation, after all.[14] All skills are gifts from Him who gives freely out of pure, fatherly, divine goodness and mercy. When those who engage in higher education learn about how the world works, they are learning more, not less, about the God who stands behind it all.

By locating the work of professionals in this larger narrative context, preachers cultivate in their hearers three fundamental Christian characteristics. First, the larger narrative helps professionals grow in thanksgiving. Above all, they give thanks for the forgiveness of sins and eternal life that comes through faith in Jesus. They also learn to give thanks to God for the human capacity to learn, grow, and advance in knowledge. Second, this gratitude leads to humility. Professionals (like all people) are creatures whose existence and ability are entirely contingent upon the Creator. Any good they are able to accomplish has its source in the One who gave them everything and works through them in hidden ways. Third, this narrative context helps professionals recognize the penultimate nature of their contributions to human flourishing. We live in a time of expectation for Christ to return and make all things new. The good that we are able to accomplish in the meantime—the healing, the justice, the meaningful support—will always be incomplete. But positive steps *can* be taken, and when they are, preachers help professionals recognize such contributions as glimpses of the final restoration to come.

13 For more details about preaching the biblical narrative, see David R. Schmitt, "Telling God's Story," in *Concordia Journal* 40, no. 2 (Spring 2014): 101–12 and Joel P. Okamoto, "The Word of the Cross and the Story of Everything," in *Concordia Journal* 45, no. 3 (Summer 2019): 51–66.

14 To paraphrase Augustine, all truth is God's truth. See *On Christian Doctrine* 2.18.28, where he writes, "Let every good and true Christian understand that wherever truth may be found, it belongs to his Master" (tr. by James Shaw, in *A Select Library of Nicene and Post-Nicene Fathers of the Christian Church*, First Series, ed. Philip Schaff, [Buffalo, NY: Christian Literature Publishing Co., 1887], 2:545).

Ethics Properly Framed

Among the helpful contributions to Christian theology made by Martin Luther is a distinction known as the two kinds of righteousness.[15] This distinction recognizes that all human beings were made to be in relationships—both with God and with other people. To be fully human, Luther said, is to be rightly related (or, righteous) in both directions.

The problem is that sin has diminished our humanity and disrupted both types of relationships. It has separated us from God *and* estranged us from one another. The good news is that God makes us right with Himself through the promise of forgiveness, life, and salvation. All who repent and believe in Jesus receive the first kind of righteousness through faith alone (Romans 10:17; Ephesians 2:8–9; Philippians 3:9). Closely related to this is the second kind of righteousness. This refers to the way we treat one another in light of being made right with God. He instructs His forgiven people to be forgiving people who give of themselves to make things right in their relationships with others. Robert Kolb and Charles Arand explain, "As social creatures, we have been fashioned by God to live in a social web of mutually constitutive relationships, in which we not only receive life and support from others but also contribute to the life and well-being of others."[16]

The distinction between two kinds of righteousness is helpful for preachers as they address professionals and their sense of ethical responsibility. It enables the preacher to affirm the use of vocational skills for the good of others *and* the ethical codes that provide boundaries. For example, preachers encourage judges to love their neighbor by making just decisions. They encourage teachers to love their neighbor by employing effective pedagogical techniques. They encourage financial advisors to love their neighbor by helping them invest ethically and shrewdly. The theological principle undergirding this affirmation of ethical behavior is the idea that God's law is good. Not only does

15 For a helpful introduction to this distinction, see Robert Kolb and Charles P. Arand, *The Genius of Luther's Theology: A Wittenberg Way of Thinking for the Contemporary Church* (Grand Rapids, MI: Baker Academic, 2008), 21–128.

16 Kolb and Arand, *The Genius of Luther's Theology*, 54.

God's law reveal our need for forgiveness. It also guides us to order our relationships rightly. As preachers proclaim God's twofold command to love God above all else and love our neighbor as ourselves, they provide a solid foundation for professionals to follow and even exceed the ethical standards of their profession.

The two kinds of righteousness distinction also provides a more stable foundation from which to answer questions left unanswered by ethical codes of conduct. Why should we treat others ethically? We love our neighbor because God has first loved us. He has sent us to love others in His name. When professionals offer their skill and insight to care for others, they are participating in His work of caring for creation.[17] This also answers the question "How?" We love our neighbors by fulfilling our vocations in ways that are consistent with the apostolic testimony in the New Testament. Even as ethical standards change with changing laws, the Scriptures provide an external standard that remains constant. The Hippocratic oath is an example of a professional code that is consistent with God's command that we "fear and love God, so that we neither endanger nor harm the lives of our neighbors, but instead help and support them in all of life's needs."[18]

Security Properly Grounded

All people search for personal security. This is necessary in a dangerous and uncertain world. While they are not alone in this search, professionals are tempted to put too much confidence in earthly sources of security because it seems more closely within reach. Indeed, the more "successful" professionals become, the more tempted they are to find security in the temporal gifts of God. This not only distracts them from God's eternal promises. It can also prevent them from recognizing the needs of their neighbors.

17 The Lutheran Confessions go to great lengths to emphasize the necessity of preaching and teaching good works—not for salvation but for the benefit of the neighbor. See, for example, the Augsburg Confession, Article XX, on faith and good works, as well as the Apology of the Augsburg Confession IV 136 on justification, which says, "We openly confess, therefore, that the keeping of the law must begin in us and then increase more and more. And we include both simultaneously, namely, the inner spiritual impulses and the outward good works. Therefore the opponents' claims are false when they charge that our people do not teach about good works since our people not only require them but also show how they can be done" (Kolb-Wengert).

18 Kolb-Wengert, Small Catechism, Fifth Commandment.

While there are many candidates in a professional's interminable search for security—including their own ability, the social status their work provides, and even the work ethic that enables them to succeed—perhaps the most common is wealth. Luther called money "the most common idol on earth."[19] This is why we need to experience three types of conversions: one of the heart, one of the mind, and one of the purse.[20] Jesus was thinking along the same lines in Luke 12:16–21. There He issued a warning about coveting the possessions of others. To make His point, He told a story about a man who had made plans to build bigger and better barns to store his great wealth. (A professional's investment portfolio might be the present-day equivalent.) Secure in his wealth, the man set out to "relax, eat, drink, and be merry" (v. 19). But that night God came to him and said, "Fool! This night your soul is required of you, and the things you have prepared, whose will they be?" (v. 20). The security his wealth provided was an illusion.

As noted above, professionals who have accumulated great wealth and social status have reasons both for thanksgiving and caution. The preacher can help with both. These are gifts from God to be received with thanksgiving. But they are also fragile. As the man in the parable learned, wealth cannot protect professionals against that which makes us ultimately insecure, namely, death. The same goes for the security we seek in social standing. A lifetime of "successful" service in any vocation can be canceled in a flash with a moral failure or an unexpected market swing.

The search for personal security also becomes a problem when the security remains only personal. The point of Jesus' parable in Luke 12 was not about giving. But it is worth noting that the man who built the barns was focused on keeping everything for himself. Rather than giving generously and sharing with those in need, he sought to strengthen the security of his own position. This temptation for professionals is strong. Their grip on sources of earthly security grows tighter in proportion to the sacrifices they have made to achieve it.

19 Large Catechism I 7.

20 A saying widely but spuriously attributed to Martin Luther.

How ought preachers to address the professional's search for personal security? They should speak honestly about temptations to find security in anything other than the promises of God in Christ. Financial abundance and social status offer only an illusion of security. It is better for professionals to learn that in advance rather than to founder when moth and rust (and death) destroy. Preachers also call their hearers to focus their attention on making the lives of their neighbors more secure through giving to those who are in need. As masks through whom God provides for the needs of all people, professionals have the privilege of helping others achieve a variety of forms of temporal and earthly security.

These warnings and commands cannot be the preacher's only word about security. The preacher is especially called to proclaim the promises that God offers through faith in Christ. These promises, which will be realized in full at the return of Jesus, are the only source of true and lasting security. They are grounded in His resurrection from the dead, which is the only source and foundation of the Christian faith and life.[21] In the name of the risen Lord, preachers proclaim the promise of eternal joy and peace that will characterize life in the new creation when Jesus returns. They call their hearers to give thanks for the forgiveness, life, and salvation that are theirs through faith in Jesus. And they encourage professionals to risk their own temporary security for the sake of their neighbor who needs their loving service.

21 See 1 Corinthians 15:12–20.

PART 2

PROFESSIONS *as* VOCATIONS

THE HEART OF THE COUNSELOR

Margaret Christmas Thomas

Dr. Margaret Christmas Thomas, LMFT, LMHC, NCC, is a Professor in and Dean of the Townsend Institute at Concordia University Irvine. She was instrumental in starting Concordia's counseling program. Prior to coming to Concordia, she led national counseling and academic services for the world's largest human services provider and consulted internationally in the areas of counseling, education, and special education services.

> For to us a child is born, to us a son is given; and the government shall be upon His shoulder, and His name shall be called Wonderful Counselor, Mighty God, Everlasting Father, Prince of Peace.
>
> *Isaiah 9:6*

Introduction

In this chapter we will explore two questions. First, what does it mean to be called as a counselor? And second, how does Christ's example of the "Wonderful Counselor" and "Prince of Peace" resonate in the hearts of those who pursue this calling?

First, let us identify our audience. The terminology for the helping professions has changed significantly since psychology first emerged as a science in the late nineteenth century. As our understanding has grown, so have our specialties and derivations. Its children are many, and I would consider my brothers and sisters numerous: marriage and family therapists, social workers, mental health counselors, licensed professional counselors, and licensed psychologists. This family of professions is often broadly called psychotherapists in state statute. But the calling even extends to our kindred: school counselors, addictions professionals, psychiatrists, and pastoral counselors. New specialties are cropping up constantly as our understanding deepens. Many of us, like me, belong to two or more within our genre, and some even to other professions like the medical and pastoral fields.

At heart, we all resonate and respond to a special call expressed in

Proverbs 20:5: "The purpose in a man's heart is like deep water, but a man of understanding will draw it out." We facilitate the heart work; we seek to ease the mind and spirit. In my national and international work, I came to see firsthand a vast army engaged in this work of mercy. In a timeframe of just one month, I saw social workers helping with children at a converted orphanage in New York, vocational counselors in Puerto Rico ending generational poverty by humbly teaching teenage fathers a trade that would give them dignity in their community and means to support their families, licensed professional counselors in the Blue Ridge Mountains helping sexual trauma victims end a cycle of pain and deprivation, and licensed psychologists in Arizona working with veterans suffering from PTSD and the internal pain expressed externally to their families. God works through all of these helping professionals to bring healing to the psyche. The Christians among them are part of what C. S. Lewis described as the "big C" Church, a mighty army established by God and sent to every time and place;[1] they are moved especially by God's love in Christ to use their professional training to bring the love and healing of Christ to the hurting. In this chapter, we delve further into this very special vocational call.

God Prepares the Soil

Many of us find this calling through our own pain and struggle. When I entered my formal counseling training at the University of Central Florida, one of my professors shared that over 60 percent of students go into counseling because they themselves have overcome some form of trauma or pain. This is a good thing if we work out our own issues sufficiently before we enter the professional phase of our careers. Just as the twelve tribes of Israel set up twelve stones as a reminder to future generations that God brought them through the Jordan River into the Promised Land (Joshua 4), so we can help others work toward a more flourishing future. If we are careful to check our own baggage, so to speak, before we enter practice, then we who have experienced God's love and healing can serve as living reminders to others of God's goodness. As an educator and leader in creating one of the largest counseling

1 See C. S. Lewis, *The Screwtape Letters* (New York: The Macmillan Company, 1948), 15.

training programs in the country, I can testify that many people go into the field for just this reason. They have turned their stumbling stones into stepping stones and want to do so for others. As surely as God works all things for good, He has worked in you to turn your pain into a stepping stone not only for you but also for others.

Regardless of what in your background led you to discover your desire to be a counselor—whether it was something you always felt called to do or something you found later in life—the role of self-care and proactive growth is imperative to be a healthy healer. Sometimes the gifts we are given can cut both ways when we have not been caring for ourselves. The sensitivity, advanced empathy, and ability for deep analysis necessary for our work may cause us to be especially vulnerable to some of the very suffering we seek to heal in others. Ensuring that you know what heals you and taking the time for yourself to be refreshed is scriptural (Genesis 2:2–3). Paying attention to your own spiritual care by regularly hearing God's Word, confessing sins, and being reminded of God's forgiveness ensures you are ministered to so that you can reboot each week and serve others. Healthy life habits such as time in Scripture, mental and physical rest each day, exercise, and a rich prayer life are all a part of being an effective practitioner.

Similarly, for the sake of our own health, we need to know our own boundaries and where we begin and end in relation to God's work in others. Counselors have been called to love our neighbor in a very distinctive and profoundly personal way. We provide a safe place where many will uncover their deepest sadness, fears, hopes, and dreams, and we often do this daily for many people one after another. Where does one find the energy if not from the ageless Fount? This is a profound mystery that for me as a mature professional was humbling to realize. Rest in the knowledge that just as God calls us to our vocations, He also equips us for them (Ephesians 2:10), providing us with the heart, inclination, and refreshment to do our work. An entire book could be devoted to just this one point for counselors, and I encourage you to seek out such resources for tending to your own mental, spiritual, and physical health so that you can live out your calling and be fortified to accomplish it.

Vocation in Context

Vocation is one of my favorite theological concepts and has been incredibly rewarding in my own life. One of the great privileges of the helping professions is that we equip those we serve for their vocations (or help them discover them). The counselor's role often includes guiding others, even apart from mental health issues, as leaders in agencies and organizations (including higher education) through the lens of understanding people. When I think about the definition of vocation, I love Gene Edward Veith's description: "God teaches through teachers; He protects us through the vocations of police officers, firefighters, soldiers, and government officials; He brings beauty through artists; He proclaims His Word and administers His Sacraments through pastors."[2] In reading biblical passages such as 1 Corinthians 7:17 and 12:4–31, Martin Luther realized that "every Christian is called to particular offices and tasks, through which God Himself works to govern and care for His created order."[3] Through our calling as counselors we are the masks that God wears to quietly and continually care for His creation. In effect, your service isn't simply between you and the person you serve but also about God caring for His creation through you and caring for you through His creation.

As you no doubt have experienced as a counselor, just because it is your calling does not mean it will always be easy, and we do not always do it perfectly or even well all of the time. Remember Moses, with a speech impediment, whom God used to stir a nation, or even David, a man after God's own heart, but a sinner as well? The roll call of faith in Hebrews 11 is filled with imperfect people God has used before us. It is worth remembering whenever we fall short of our vocations that there is complete forgiveness in Christ. This renews us daily to continue on with our callings to fulfill them well for others. When we give glory to God, it also helps us to connect to something deeper that in turn deepens us. There is freedom in recognizing the work of the Holy Spirit. He gives us the privilege to be His hands and feet, but in the end, as a salve against both our arrogance and our self-effacement, we remember

2 Gene Edward Veith, "God at Work," *Lutheran Witness* 120, no. 7 (July 2001): 12.

3 Gene Edward Veith, "God at Work," 12.

that the work of the Holy Spirit will not begin or end with us. Have faith that the same God who began the good work in you (and even placed the dream of it in your heart) will see it through to completion. It is a great privilege to live these callings out, even if it isn't always easy. We are not always ready when we begin. In times when it feels like you have fallen short, meditate on Philippians 1:6, where Paul writes, "And I am sure of this, that He who began a good work in you will bring it to completion at the day of Jesus Christ."

Connection to My Call

I felt called early in my career to be a counselor—the honest truth is that I have always been a counselor. Even though I have been the principal leading incredible teams of educators in some really tough schools while getting my degree and licensure, served in both national and international counseling leadership roles, and consulted with foreign ministries in counseling and academics, I have at heart remained true to that call. Even as a leader at Concordia University Irvine, as a professor, and as an administrator, my call is always close at hand. I think the unique set of gifts God gave to me helped me to see systems and to carry out my work in loving service to others and to His glory.

It is important to think carefully about how we as members of this profession advocate for it and for those we are called to serve. I would like to share the story of Concordia University Irvine's counseling program. In 2014, I had been out of my professional environment for a while after getting married, having my daughter, and moving across the country. I have always loved the open-hearted nature of the counseling profession and looked forward to our professional conferences, a time to fellowship with kindred spirits, who are often exceedingly nurturing and quick to embrace diversity with open arms. When I went back to the American Counseling Association conference that year, I was deeply troubled by some of the changes that had occurred and what had become normal in the profession. The paradigm had shifted so that rather than acceptance of fringe viewpoints, those viewpoints seemed to be the only ones for which there was room any longer. Some of the keynote speakers gave advice—calling it "innovative techniques"—that would have been truly harmful to any vulnerable family in my church. Their advice was deeply troubling and contrary to Scripture—for example, that it is fine to have an open marriage or for children to experiment in detrimental ways. Knowing what I know about families from a professional and personal standpoint, I understand that families go through very vulnerable seasons. If one of my church families were to go to one of these counselors and receive such advice, I would love to think they would have the wisdom to discern the difference. But how much better if they had somewhere safe to go? When I returned from that conference I spoke to the provosts about the possibility for Concordia to begin a counseling program infused both with Christian wisdom and best-in-class counseling techniques. This unique program was launched a few years later in 2017 in partnership with Dr. John Townsend. It is a tremendous blessing as a university to be able to train and equip counselors to serve Christian and non-Christian people during vulnerable seasons of their lives, to wield considerable skill and wisdom serving secular and religious sectors. I believe over time our program will have the opportunity to influence the face of an entire profession. You, too, have had or will have opportunities to shape your client's lives, train interns, and influence institutions you are a part of just by your presence and by the work of the Holy Spirit, just as He worked through Daniel, a capable and competent adviser to the king of a very secular society (Daniel 2:48). I want to encourage you to recognize your influence and the work of the Holy Spirit through you. I do not know what the future holds, but I know in whose hand the future is held, and I know whose hand is holding yours too.

It is important to linger a moment to recognize that our vocation extends beyond church settings. Just as an emergency department doctor is called to serve everyone who comes through the door, we are also often called as Christians to serve in secular settings. The creed of those we serve does not change our work, and they do not have to pass a test for us to serve them. They, too, whether they know it or not, are created in the image of God and redeemed by the blood of Christ. As Mother Teresa once said, they are Jesus in disguise. We are called to serve, allowing God the Holy Spirit to call and work in others. So as we counsel people in difficult seasons, regardless of their background or creed, we live out all our callings, giving glory to God and enjoying the pleasure of being the mask of God to others. Our joy can be found as we participate in God's care for the people He created.

Living Out Your Calling

We have talked about how we are called and the right thinking about the work of our calling. Now I want to talk about how we live out our calling. Sometimes the day-to-day can erode our passion. At worst we may be confronted with ethical conflicts within the systems where we work. Maybe it is the fifth year or the fiftieth, but sooner or later we can be weary of the same thing day in and day out or the conflict inherent in human-made systems. So as you live out your calling each day, I have two questions for you. First, what do you love? Second, what do you stand for? These questions will follow you throughout your career. More than once in my life, deep decisions have hinged on the answers to those two questions. Our vocation is our love made visible. If you love people or counseling, social work or psychotherapy, that will become visible through your life. I want to encourage you to be bold, love deeply, and stand strong in your beliefs. It is not necessary that you "win" with every client in a broken world, because in the end you will not be judged by the world. In the end you will be judged by God. He knows your heart, He gave His Son for you, and it is He who works through you with every client.

Sooner or later we all have to confront the reality that we are working in our calling in a broken world. Throughout my career, as you may have already done and certainly will in the future, I have had to stand up for the ideals I believe in. When I was working as an international consultant in Bahrain, I was moving the girls juvenile justice system from the Ministry of Police to the Ministry of Social Work. Before I left the United States, my vice president briefed me to prepare me for the circumstances of these girls' appalling situation. I had a lot of domestic experience working with at-promise and at-risk youth, many of whom had interfaced with juvenile justice. What I was not prepared for in this specific case was how these young girls got into juvenile justice. A review of the case files shocked me—in many cases, they were actually the victims of abuse perpetrated by authority figures, and yet they were blamed for it. They had been abandoned to the justice system and left in residential detention centers for years. It was all they knew, and they believed it was their fault.

The people at the facility certainly believed it was their fault—they were "bad" or had brought circumstances on themselves even at tender elementary ages—but when I saw the girls I only saw their desperation. In moving them from police custodial care into a social work atmosphere, I designed programs to help reunite them with their families, work with their self-esteem, and introduce a therapeutic model that did not focus on blaming the victim. While these are pretty standard in the United States, this was all new for the people I was working with, and often it was not received well. It did not help that my name was Dr. Christmas—sometimes in the conversations, my having a different religion than the other persons was used against me. But no amount of fear, scorn, or any other barrier was going to keep me from working to help these girls have something better. I could easily have walked away. No one would have blamed me, especially after a headline one morning read, "Woman Killed after Found Driving Unauthorized." In the end, they offered for me to stay beyond the design and implementation phase that I had come for. I counted that as progress, though not a victory until those girls re-entered regular life with a future. Since I was about to be married, I chose not to work apart from my soon-to-be husband so early in our marriage. (I could write another whole book on how our various callings can sometimes lead us in different dizzying directions![4]) Thankfully, the family reintegration system, vocational training, and program design I had implemented remained even after I returned home.

You, too, will come up against systems that, for whatever reason, are simply not fair. As gifted, caring professionals, you may have

4 See Nancy Stoehr's essay "The Vocation of Pharmacist" in this volume for one example of a conflict between vocations.

opportunities to take on the hard case, run a difficult program, care for a belligerent patient, serve in a dangerous part of the world, or encounter systems that are far from perfect. What will you do when you encounter these choices? Will you say, "This is how it has always been. I cannot change it, so why try?" Will you become so offended that you cannot do even a little good if it cannot be perfect? Will you carve out a safe place and bury your talents so that you can return them to God one day unused and without want or wear (Matthew 25:14–30)? It is at these moments I want to encourage you to think back on the answer to those two questions. What do you love, and what do you stand for? Know the answer to these questions ahead of time, because it will be tested in large and small ways as you continue to live out your calling.

I was lucky in that I had a frame of reference for a different paradigm when I designed the program that I constructed for the Ministry of Social Work. Sometimes you do not. Sometimes you are in uncharted waters. One thing that has never failed me no matter how deep the waters is to pray to God for wisdom. He has always given it to me. I am no theologian like some other authors in this book, but in my experience, God has not only given me wisdom but it has been His great delight to do so (James 1:5)! He loves to confound the lofty. I am a first-generation college student and at-risk kid by any account. When I started college, I truly think I did not understand (well, "care" is probably a better word) exactly what a GPA was. God loves to give wisdom. Ask Him and seek Him. There was no reason for me to be consulting with foreign government agencies over national programs, helping to develop and lead one of the nation's largest counseling programs, or even to get a doctorate in the first place. I cannot count the tears or the prayers for wisdom, from humble beginnings to the luxuries of diplomatic-area accommodations (and everything in between). But God has.

In closing, I would like to leave you with a couple of final thoughts. First, in relation to those you serve, remember that you serve a hurting world that, no matter how much you pour in, will still be hurting when you leave it. This is especially important for counselors who may sometimes only see parts of the growth of an individual. Consider these words by Theodore Roosevelt:

> The credit belongs to the man who is actually in the arena, whose face is marred by dust and sweat and blood; who strives valiantly; who errs, who comes short again and again, because there is no effort without error and shortcoming; but who does actually strive to do the deeds; who knows great enthusiasms, the great devotions; who spends himself in a worthy cause; who at the best knows, in the end, the triumph of high achievement, and who at the worst, if he fails, at least fails while daring greatly, so that his place shall never be with those cold and timid souls who neither know victory nor defeat.[5]

Second, remember that our profession and its rules and laws ultimately must bow to higher truth, one that we do not fully comprehend even at our pinnacle. Do we exalt our profession as the final truth, or is there something deeper than the reality we have constructed? Our field is deeply connected to the heart and the psyche and is also rooted in healing. Just as the DSM is a subsection of the ICD, counseling is a part of the larger clinical realm. Precisely because of our imperfect understanding as human beings, we have created a system of psychopathology and diagnosis to more completely attempt to understand the totality of the human mind and its brokenness. While it is worthy and good to seek understanding, let us never forget in our journey that our classifications at their root are arbitrary agreements that we as professionals use to communicate clusters of symptomatology with one another. A gifted practitioner may spend decades perfecting understanding of that diagnostic system, may use it to accomplish many good works and have the privilege of healing many souls that God has entrusted to the practitioner's care, but it is and always will remain a human-made system temporally defined.

5 Theodore Roosevelt, "Citizenship in a Republic" (address given at the Sorbonne in Paris, France, April 23, 1910), https://www.presidency.ucsb.edu/documents/address-the-sorbonne-paris-france-citizenship-republic (accessed October 21, 2023).

Let us never forget that God sees us in the context of totality, and these lines we draw, while useful now and worthy of grave consideration and study, are only lines. "For now we see in a mirror dimly, but then face to face. Now I know in part; then I shall know fully, even as I have been fully known" (1 Corinthians 13:12). As you discover the range and variety of God's creation in the human mind through your daily work, as well as the brokenness of our fallen world, do not be afraid to explore deeply and expound mightily. But when you finish your journey always remember this passage: "For I am sure that neither death nor life, nor angels nor rulers, nor things present nor things to come, nor powers, nor height nor depth, nor anything else in all creation, will be able to separate us from the love of God in Christ Jesus our Lord" (Romans 8:38–39).

Finally, I want to leave you with the assurance that God will continue to guide and bless you as you live out your calling as a counselor. He has equipped you for that to which He has called you. I also want to challenge you to know what you stand for and to love boldly. One day when you look back after a long and satisfying career, I hope that you will see how God worked through you to serve others. Thank you for being a force for healing in the hearts and minds of those you serve. Please know that you are a part of a vast army of professionals all over the world working for healing and growth in the minds and hearts of the suffering. You are the image of God to a hurting world, modeled after the one who is Himself the Prince of Peace and Wonderful Counselor.

FAITH IN NURSING: APPLYING GOD'S WORD

Terry Cottle

Dr. Terry Cottle, RN, CNS, served as Associate Professor of Nursing and Assistant Director of the Nursing Department at Concordia University Irvine until her retirement. During her tenure at Concordia, she taught in accelerated BSN, RN to BSN, and MSN programs. Before coming to Concordia, she worked in a variety of hospitals and healthcare settings in San Bernardino and Orange Counties, CA.

When considering the concept of the vocation of nursing, it is important to understand what it means to be a nurse. Nurses are taught from the beginning of their studies that nursing is both an art and a science. The science part is easily understood; nurses diligently study to develop the core scientific knowledge necessary to apply the skills and competencies needed for the role of healthcare provider. Through study in the liberal arts, nurses learn of the holistic nature of individuals; they develop an understanding of the physical, mental, emotional, spiritual, and cultural aspects of those who are in need of the many aspects of healthcare. Instrumental to nursing is Florence Nightingale, who is largely recognized as the founder and inspiration for the profession of nursing. She is known as "the Lady with the Lamp," which developed from her nursing work in field hospitals where she carried a kerosene lamp to check on her patients. That image has provided the description of her work as shining light into the lonelier and darker places where she found those in need of care. She began her work in the late 1800s, and although she faced opposition from the leaders at the time, she developed and promoted the concept that the purpose of nursing is to serve others and to serve all who need care (Peate, 2016).

Nurses are taught to understand and embrace the values and ideals of the profession. To meet these moral obligations, nurses are encouraged to develop and incorporate into their personal and professional lives the virtues of wisdom, patience, compassion, altruism, honesty, courage, knowledge, and skill. According to the American Nurses Association Code of Ethics, these virtues are necessary to promote the core values of well-being, human dignity, health, independence, and respect (ANA, 2015).

Studying nursing at a Christian university has many benefits. A major benefit in coping with today's society is the reinforcement and application of God's promises found in the Bible. Jesus tells us in John 16:33, "I have said these things to you, that in Me you may have peace. In the world you will have tribulation. But take heart; I have overcome the world." Nurses often care for people in their lowest moments, with disease or trauma, many times with no cures. Patients and families who struggle to make sense of the situation they find themselves in, trying to understand the purpose or reason for disease or disability or even death, will try to find peace, or at least acceptance. Trusting in God's promise found in Philippians 3:21 that He will "transform our lowly body to be like His glorious body" is often a great comfort. When the patient's time on this earth is ending, the promise of John 3:16 can bring relief: "For God so loved the world, that He gave His only Son, that whoever believes in Him should not perish but have eternal life."

The words of Ecclesiastes 3 were incorporated into a folk song in the 1960s and provide a calming way to express the belief that "for everything there is a season, and a time for every matter under heaven: a time to be born, and a time to die; a time to plant, and a time to pluck up what is planted" (Ecclesiastes 3:1–2). Faith and trust in God and His promises provide a foundation for nurses' holistic care, which, by definition, attends to the physical, mental, emotional, spiritual, and environmental aspects of health. Nursing research shows life satisfaction and hope for the future is associated with the spiritual well-being of the patient. O'Brien (2019) explains further that people who report a high degree of spiritual contentment and personal faith were more positive and satisfied with their lives, even when suffering from illnesses. Mauk and Hobus (2021) report several studies that demonstrate a correlation between spiritual health and a reduction in pain, depression, and risk for suicide.

Christian nurses understand that they are equipped to serve in the nursing profession because God leads their path. They recognize the dignity of all humans who have been created in the image of God. Christian nurses also recognize that who they are is defined by the fact that, first and foremost, they belong to Jesus and that, second, they are to care for others. Knowledge of the science of health combined with faith and a spiritual understanding allows nurses to embody the virtues, values, and moral obligations of the nursing profession.

Lutheran Vocation in Nursing

The idea of a Lutheran vocation in nursing correlates to the promises found in God's Word. As Christians, we rely on God and His promises for the world. We trust that He is in every situation in life. We also have the opportunity to live the greatest commandments as given to us by Jesus Christ: "You shall love the Lord your God with all your heart and with all your soul and with all your mind and with all your strength. . . . You shall love your neighbor as yourself" (Mark 12:30–31). With an understanding of the purpose of vocation as loving and serving one's neighbor, we can clearly see that nursing truly is a vocation, a service to God. When we realize that God has called us to serve our neighbors, not abstractly love humanity, then we recognize the way nurses are called to serve the real human beings placed in our paths.

Martin Luther explains vocation as God working through us. It is important to recognize that God is still active in the lives of those He created. God is active in the spiritual realm, specifically through His Word and Sacraments. God is active in the earthly realm, through the actions of all people. We are created for a purpose and have been given gifts that allow us to fulfill that purpose in our lives. Veith (2021) explains that we are able to live our purpose as a result of our God-given gifts, talents, opportunities, and stations. God affects the lives of those He created on a daily basis, minute by minute, by working through us, our vocations, and our desire to serve Him. This means God's work of caring for the human race is accomplished through the work of other human beings. Indeed, God has created human beings with a variety of talents and provided the opportunity for those human beings to live out their vocations using those talents to care for one another. This means God has provided nurses with the ability to understand the science of nursing, the strength to work as part of a healthcare team providing needed care, and the opportunity to demonstrate His love to those in need. By recognizing and following the direction of our God-given talents, we are able to serve other people in the capacity most needed. Luther calls the various occupations "masks of God" where we, in our vocations, are the channels of the ongoing care God provides (Veith, 2021). Likewise, Mother Teresa referred to herself as a pencil used by the hand of God. She believed that the work she was able to do was through the power of God working through her (Poplin, 2008). This is an important concept—God works through all people, bestowing different abilities that lead to different vocations. That means all of us serve and are served by one another. This is reflected in the diversity of roles on a healthcare team: we all have a role on the team to serve and care for our patients, our communities, and one another. This is vocation in nursing, using God-given talents to care for other people, our neighbors, as we are trained to do and as we are called to do.

It is important to understand that vocation in nursing is about the relationship between the nurse and God's call to serve His purpose. This is important to understand for nurses whose roles may change throughout their career. Most nurses begin their careers providing hands-on care to individual patients. This makes obvious the concept of being used in God's hand like a pencil, as nurses' hands are used to provide needed healthcare. When taking on other nursing roles such as leadership, research, or educational positions, this vocation takes on a slightly different form. In these roles, the idea of serving God's purpose shifts to a broader definition of the neighbor we are called to serve. Instead of the single patient, the direction of our vocation becomes the healthcare team under our leadership, those who will benefit from our research, or the education that provides others the opportunity to practice their own vocations. These additional roles are also a result of God-given talents designed to allow us to live out our vocation and fulfill our purpose of serving others. In whatever role, it is indeed standing on holy ground, for ourselves as we live out our vocation and for our neighbors as the recipients of our service.

Christian nurses can certainly rely on the promises in God's Word to provide comfort for themselves as well as their patients, families, and colleagues. Understanding the vocation of nursing can encourage nurses on a daily basis to continue the challenging work of serving those in need of their care. However, nurses often face ethically challenging situations in healthcare, with patients and families, with colleagues, with organizations, and in society. The nurse must be prepared to participate in identifying ethical solutions in a variety of situations. How does the Word of God or the call to follow Jesus aid the nurse in these situations? It is important to understand that the vocation of nursing is not just about the work nurses do; it encompasses who they are and how they are. Veith (2002) refers to this as the theology of the Christian life. Christian nurses respond to the call from God to serve His people and all people, and as a result, Christian nurses have additional standards for serving.

Ethics in Nursing

Nurses are often the first healthcare worker to recognize an ethical situation at the bedside or at their workplace and are able to use their knowledge of ethical theories to support decision-making in healthcare situations. There are many theories available to guide the nurse in an ethical dilemma, which can often make the process of finding solutions more difficult. In response to the many professional ethical dilemmas faced by nurses, two trusted nursing organizations, the American Nurses Association (ANA) and the International Council of Nurses (ICN), developed guidelines for support. These guidelines inform the nursing profession of the expectations of considering ethical obligations while providing quality care. The ANA Code of Ethics (2015) is described as a promise to healthcare teams and consumers that nurses will do their best to support one another in providing care in such a way that all nurses can practice ethically in meeting professional obligations.

The ICN Code of Ethics (2021) includes expectations for nursing education to include teaching on ethical issues and decision-making. This guideline further encourages teaching on the importance of social action, informed consent, confidentiality, privacy, beneficence, maleficence, and professional values.

Applied ethics—the practice of using ethical frameworks to provide justifiable solutions in difficult clinical situations—allows the healthcare team to determine appropriately ethical actions. When using applied ethics to determine appropriate and justifiable actions, it is often necessary to identify the legal and religious components of the situation. Nurses are taught the many laws surrounding healthcare and are encouraged to understand religious beliefs so as to be able to assist in the decision-making. Nurses are taught to respect the belief systems of those they care for by first understanding their own beliefs and recognizing how these beliefs may influence the way they provide care or assist in decision-making. Belief systems provide structure in developing our own values. They are designed to provide explanations for such issues as good and evil, life and death, and health and illness, and they typically include an ethical component that directs and defines appropriate behaviors. Religion often provides the foundation for personal belief systems and their guidance in behaviors and decision-making. Christian nurses typically consider their own religious beliefs when confronted with ethical issues, and while this may provide the nurse with personal support for decisions, these nurses recognize others may not have the same beliefs. The ANA Code of Ethics (2015) addresses the potential for conflicts of interest by acknowledging the challenges of contradictory expectations as well as conflicts between personal, professional, and others' values. The guidelines direct the nurse to address these conflicts in ways that support their own beliefs while ensuring safe, quality care.

It is often thought that belief systems provided explanations for events that science was not able to explain. Many people believe advances in science and technology have provided answers to the questions that belief systems traditionally addressed. However, although science can explain many phenomena previously considered unexplainable, technological advances have created situations where people may feel an increased need for religious belief systems to assist in making difficult decisions. For example, advances in genetic testing can determine if an infant will have certain life-altering diseases, which might influence the parents to terminate the pregnancy. Technology has certainly allowed very preterm infants to survive, very ill people to live only by artificial means, and people in general to live to much older ages than ever before. Indeed, science and technological advances have provided for advanced knowledge and skills, but making decisions on the appropriate use of these advancements is still guided by personal and professional ethics. The ethical principles of autonomy, nonmaleficence, beneficence, justice, confidentiality, veracity, and fidelity provide guidance in many healthcare decisions. In addition, nurses are ethically required to protect those who are unable to protect themselves. However, decisions are not always easily made and are made more difficult when considering the emotions that usually accompany such decisions.

Consider this case. Alicia has been an RN for over 35 years; she is currently working in administration after receiving her doctorate in nursing leadership. She considers herself fortunate to have great relationships with her in-laws and spends as much time with them as possible. Her mother-in-law, Bertha, discussed her end-of-life wishes with the family and developed the appropriate documents to support her wishes. Her advance directive indicated no intubation, IV fluids, or other life-prolonging measures to be used. Alicia was called upon one weekend to take Bertha to the emergency department by the daughter who held the healthcare power of attorney but had plans to be out of the area and would be unreachable by phone. The daughter stated Bertha seemed confused and was difficult to understand. Upon assessment by the ED physician, it was determined that Bertha had a urinary tract infection and dehydration contributing to the confusion and that both of these could easily be managed by IV fluids and antibiotics. Alicia agreed and the treatment was initiated. When the daughter returned, she was quite upset by the treatment that had been provided and pointed out on the advance directive where it stated no IV fluids. Alicia explained her reasoning that it was not a life-saving measure at this point but rather a treatment for an infection.

What do you think? In such situations, which ethical principle is most important? Beneficence would suggest that good be done, and nonmaleficence requires that no harm be done: treatment was provided for the good, but was harm done when considering the advance directive? While Alicia believed she was using professional judgment and fidelity to allow treatment, was she discounting Bertha's autonomy as stated in the advance directive? As is the case with many healthcare situations, decisions often become ethically fraught even when using ethical theories to assist in the decision process. When making decisions such as this, rather than a right answer, it is often the case that we consider how we felt about the decision and what we learned from it. The nurse can reflect on the call from the ICN Code of Ethics to respect human rights and recognize the customs, values, and beliefs of the patient.

While ethical principles guide healthcare workers in assisting with decision-making, relationships play an important role with nurses. Relationships are the center of nursing care and contribute to nursing ethics. An important aspect of nursing ethics is respect for the value of each individual, from patients and families to peers and colleagues. Nurses are encouraged to know and practice according to their own values and moral standards and to support others according to their own personal values in decision-making without compromising their own values. However, in a constantly changing healthcare environment, nurses are frequently involved in situations that seem to have more uncertainty than direct answers.

There are some healthcare situations that can be perceived as challenging for Christian nurses. While nurses understand the concept of a woman's right to choose the course of her own health, Christian nurses are aware of the promise that God knows, loves, and has a plan for everyone from the very beginning of our existence. How does a Christian nurse care for a patient seeking an abortion or requesting assistance to end his or her own life? Additionally, how does a Christian nurse care for the patient who has very different fundamental beliefs? First and foremost, all nurses must begin with a foundational respect for the dignity of every person. This includes their right to choose their own beliefs and to direct their own actions. While God directs His people through the parable of the Good Samaritan in Luke 10:25–37 to care for everyone as their neighbor, the Christian nurse can rely on God to direct the course of action for any situation as He promises in Matthew 10:19–20—He will provide the words to say when the time comes. In many situations, it is permissible to convey disagreement with the chosen course of action while caring for the person who made the choice. The bottom line for the Christian nurse, then, is to serve other people as professional training and personal values allow. In challenging situations, continue to trust God's love for all of His people and act accordingly, trusting in God's understanding and forgiveness for the patient and the nurse.

What Does This Mean?

For the Christian nurse, this brings us back to the idea of vocation and the defining standards for serving. Veith (2002) explains that the idea of vocation can provide direction to explain why certain actions would be right or wrong as well as provide direction for our specific roles. From the perspective of an outside observer, all nurses use the same ethical principles and standards for decision-making. It is on the inside that the idea of vocation provides direction—it is the reliance on faith to direct decision-making in difficult situations according to an understanding of God's expectations. With the understanding that vocation directs us to love and serve our neighbor and live out our faith, we can accept that God is at work within our vocations. That takes us back to the understanding that we are the "masks of God" and the pencils He uses. O'Brien (2018) writes that the work of nurses is standing on holy ground. She references Exodus 3:4–5, where God appeared to Moses in the burning bush and said, "Take your sandals off your feet, for the place on which you are standing is holy ground." When we provide care for the people God created and realize He is also present, then we recognize that we, too, are standing on holy ground. This means God is with us as we provide care and as we seek answers to ethical dilemmas. O'Brien (2018) calls this the gift and grace of our nursing vocation; we believe we are standing on holy ground, and we trust that God will bless our endeavors, forgive our mistakes for Jesus' sake, and give us peace in our decisions and actions.

References

American Nurses Association (ANA). (2015). *Code of Ethics for Nurses with Interpretive Statements.* https://www.nursingworld.org/practice-policy/nursing-excellence/ethics/code-of-ethics-for-nurses/

International Council of Nurses. (2012). *The ICN Code of Ethics for Nurses.* https://www.icn.ch/sites/default/files/2023-06/ICN_Code-of-Ethics_EN_Web.pdf

Mauk, K. L., & Hobus, M. E. (2021). *Nursing as Ministry.* Jones & Bartlett Learning.

O'Brien, M. E. (2019). *Spirituality in nursing: Standing on holy ground* (6th ed). Jones & Bartlett Learning.

Peate, I. (2016). Take a bow on 12 May. *British Journal of Nursing 25*(9), 473.

Poplin, M. (2008). *Finding Calcutta: What Mother Teresa taught me about meaningful work and service.* InterVarsity Press.

Veith, G. E., Jr. (2002). *God at work.* Crossway.

Veith, G. E., Jr. (2021). *The spirituality of the cross: The way of the first evangelicals* (3rd ed.). Concordia Publishing House.

THE VOCATION OF TEACHING

Lori B. Doyle

Sara Morgan

Dr. Lori Doyle is Associate Professor of Education, Director of the MA in Educational Leadership Program, and Assistant Director of the Servant Leadership Institute at Concordia University Irvine. She began her career as a high school English and theology teacher, taught as an adjunct professor for many years, and now enjoys her faculty role of serving a graduate student population of education professionals.

Dr. Sara Morgan is Assistant Professor of Education and Director of Special Education Credential Programs at Concordia University Irvine. She has Multiple Subjects, Education Specialist, and Administrative credentials. Her master's degree is in Special Education, and her PhD emphasis is Disability Studies. She has taught in Lutheran and public schools. Prior to moving to Concordia, she served as a Program Director for a school district in Orange County, CA.

This chapter is focused on the vocation of teaching. It is based on the perspectives of two educators, the literature and research on the field of education, and a biblical understanding of what it means to teach. Not only does the Bible have much to say on the value of children but Jesus provides a model for the importance of the role of a teacher. Many unique characteristics are associated with the teaching profession, but there are also areas of overlap with other helping professions. The reasons behind the decision to become a teacher are essential to consider, and an important aspect of a teacher's role is to be a lifelong learner. While the field of education is constantly changing, and the specific tasks associated with being a teacher might look different from one year to the next, a vocational mindset can keep one anchored in biblical truths regarding the profession.

Biblical Context

The vocation of teaching has direct links to biblical concepts and directives. The value God places on children cannot be denied (Matthew 18:10). Teaching is described by God as a gift (Romans 12:7), and Ephesians 4:12 speaks of God equipping people for works of service. In the same verse, it is the body of Christ that God would have built up through the work of people serving one another, and what a privilege it is to do this through teaching. In truth, Jesus Himself often accomplishes His work through teaching. All of this means a decision to become an educator has inherent importance.

In Mark 6:34, Jesus is described as having compassion for a large group of people, and He immediately responds by beginning to teach them many things. Jesus did not correct people who referred to Him as Rabbi or Teacher (John 3:2). He lovingly uses authority to convey information to those in need, setting an example for teachers. Romans 2:20 describes teachers as those who set an example and have knowledge to impart. While this can apply when teaching about the Bible directly, it can and absolutely does include the manner in which a teacher models biblical living through honesty, kindness, putting others first, and all the moral and ethical ways a teacher exemplifies what it means to be a shining light so that others will want to know about their loving heavenly Father (Matthew 5:16). Titus 2:7 defines the act of setting an example as doing what is good, and this is immediately followed with directions to teach with integrity.

An important concept to discuss is the connection among work, usefulness, and serving others (Ephesians 4:28). Each day, if not each minute, the vocation of teaching provides opportunities to be useful through service for the good of others in need. The School of Education at Concordia University Irvine has embraced servant leadership as the framework by which we work together and on which we base our outward actions and dealings with others. This form of leadership stems from a biblical understanding that teaching is ultimately about serving. Jesus exemplified teaching as one of many ways to serve others, and if Jesus, the greatest teacher of all, was willing to serve, then the vocation of teaching must also be defined by serving. The vocation of teaching is biblical, defined by service, and connected to the concept that work should be useful and model integrity so that, through their position of authority, teachers are shining lights in classrooms and schools.

Unique Aspects of the Profession

The uniquely complex challenges of 21st-century education can be viewed through a lens of vocation (a calling from God, through Christ, by the Holy Spirit, with others, for others). Vocation-centered educators who see their profession as a calling from God acknowledge that the same God who formed them and gave their life purpose and meaning has also equipped them for the tasks at hand, regardless of changing circumstances (Colossians 3:23–24). Vocation-centered educators who set aside self so that the work of the Lord may be accomplished do not boast about their strengths (Romans 15:18); instead, they confess that Christ's power is made perfect in their weakness (2 Corinthians 12:9). Through trials and triumphs, vocation-centered educators rely on the divine fruit of the Holy Spirit (Galatians 5:22–23). These fruits help vocation-centered educators live in community with their colleagues, encouraging one another and holding one another accountable (Hebrews 10:23–25; Philippians 2:14–16). Vocation-centered educators embrace those whom they have been called to serve. They recall that Christ came to serve and not be served (Mark 10:45), and they selflessly serve in this self-serving world. Vocation-centered educators know their calling is a gift from God to glorify God. It is not through their power but through the power of Christ, enabled by the Holy Spirit in community with and service to others (1 Peter 4:10).

With a few simple clicks on any social media platform, one can find a cacophony of perspectives about the profession. While many rightly celebrate a profession centered on working with children, the uniquely challenging aspects of teaching should be acknowledged. In addition to the long-standing frustrations of finding a balance between prepping lessons, attending a myriad of meetings (e.g., district, school site, departmental, student, parent), serving in ancillary roles, grading papers, providing meaningful feedback, responding to emails, and actually teaching, educators are experiencing new challenges. Teachers are on the front lines of a fast-changing academic, behavioral, and social-emotional landscape. Student needs, readiness, and capacity have changed (Darling-Hammond & Hyler, 2020; EAB, 2023a). The inner pandemic (see Richtel, 2022, p. 1) of mental health concerns is on the rise (EAB, 2023a; EAB, 2023b). Current political and social unrest is causing polarization, cancel culture is real, and algorithms create divisive echo chambers (Kelly, 2021). Compounding these disorienting post-COVID obstacles is a trend of destructive behavior prompted by dares on a social media platform (Heyward, 2021). These are truly unprecedented times. Or are they?

While the phrase "unprecedented times" has become common language, nothing is unprecedented to God. As the biblical author says, "What has been is what will be, and what has been done is what will be done, and there is nothing new under the sun" (Ecclesiastes 1:9). This is profound, yet somewhat unhelpful when living the daily grind. To say there is nothing new under the sun seems hopelessly blasé rather than actively engaged. However, no set of converging circumstances is unknown to God. Embracing this knowledge can provide encouragement. Teachers who embrace it can focus on being commissioned by the Creator of the universe for good work; like Esther, they have been placed in their current role "for such a time as this" (Esther 4:14). When we open ourselves to God's timing as purposeful and His provision as providential, we can embrace our calling in the right-hand kingdom, trusting that through the power of the Holy Spirit, our left-hand kingdom vocational work is the work of the Lord.

Teaching as Helping Profession

While education differs from many other fields, it overlaps with some professions, specifically those referred to as the helping professions. When asked about fields focused on serving a suffering population, one might readily think of doctors, nurses, therapists, or counselors; however, Ziaian-Ghafari and Berg (2019) discuss the potential that education professionals will also work with people experiencing psychological distress. This is not mentioned as a scare tactic to dissuade anyone from a career in teaching; it is provided as a realistic reminder that would be given to anyone entering a helping profession. It also elevates the profession in importance to consider the privileges and responsibilities associated with those who choose a career in a helping field. While teachers might not be required to stitch a physical wound, they will certainly need to tend to emotional injuries and behavioral risks in addition to the given academic challenges.

Just as nurses and counselors are advised to engage in self-care, new and experienced teachers alike are wise to think proactively about ways to maintain their own health and well-being. One suggestion is to establish a purposeful support system to include at least one person who does not work at the same school. Another idea is to set clear personal and professional boundaries. A third suggestion, backed by years of research, is to be conscious of the mediating role of self-efficacy against burnout and mental health deterioration (Saloviita & Pakarinen, 2021). Simply stated, self-efficacy refers to an employee's own perception regarding the ability to complete a task or reach an outcome (Bandura, 1982). Examples of teacher tasks might be writing lesson plans, meeting state standards, maintaining a class newsletter, meeting with parents and guardians for conferences, and following IEPs for students. Outcomes are less specific and might include developing a classroom management plan or helping students become stronger writers. Fostering self-efficacy in the small and large aspects of the profession has been shown to bolster teachers' enjoyment of and longevity in the profession. Taking advantage of professional development opportunities plays an important role in supporting teacher self-efficacy and has a positive impact, especially on new teachers, regarding motivation (Hill, 2020). The authors of this chapter each experienced many of the early challenges associated with the profession of teaching. They wished they had been more cognizant of the joys and challenges associated with entering a helping profession. They can attest to the value of advice and research on proactively working through challenges and embracing the joys of such an impactful vocation.

Personal Connections to Teaching

Teaching as a profession, and by extension the teacher as a professional, relies on a great deal of camaraderie. There is great value in having an open stance for what another educator has experienced, where their path overlaps or veers from our own, and perhaps most important, blossoming from the knowledge that we are not alone. As a way of sharing our professional journeys as educators, we, the coauthors of this chapter, would like to describe how an understanding of vocation has influenced our respective educator paths. To begin, Lori Doyle will invite you along her road, which most recently led to her serving as the Director of the Master of Arts in Educational Leadership Program at Concordia University Irvine, where her student population consists of school professionals desiring a graduate degree either in Social Emotional Learning, Character, and Ethics or in Cognition, Motivation, and Development. Following that, you will read Sara Morgan's journey from the beginning of her career in education to her current role as faculty for the teacher credential program, which allows her to work with and support undergraduate and postgraduate candidates. The authors will switch to first-person narration in order to share their personal experiences with authenticity.

I (Lori) was raised by teachers. That was the very beginning of my path toward a career in education. I lived by the school calendar, understood the schedule of a teacher, and felt like I had witnessed the highs and lows of the profession from early on. My decision to become a teacher was not without periods of time when I was sure I wanted the opposite. Can anyone relate? Around my sophomore year of college, I made the decision that it was full steam ahead for a career in secondary education. The opportunity to student teach in both public and private schools was beneficial, and I really enjoyed aspects of each. My first call was to teach high school theology and English at a Lutheran high school. Reflecting back through the lens of vocation, I understand it was not that I was fulfilling my vocation only or more so when teaching theology as opposed to English. My role as a teacher working with students from all walks of life, backgrounds, and situations and serving them through my role as their teacher was contributing to God's work in this world regardless of the subject or even the setting. The fact that my career has brought me full circle from being a classroom teacher to now supporting school professionals as they continue in the way of lifelong learning feels as much a gift as a privilege, and my admiration for teachers grows every year. As my understanding of vocation grows, so does my desire to help all education professionals recognize and embrace the joy of serving through the vocation of teaching, no matter the student population, school setting, or personal role as a school professional.

God led me (Sara) into public education. Toward the end of my undergraduate studies, I began working for a Lutheran school as an instructional assistant. I was placed in the third-grade classroom where my sister taught, and after some time, she began tasking me to serve students who needed focused help. Finding fulfillment in seeing less likely students succeed, I entered a teacher credential program to pursue a dual certificate in multiple subjects and special education. Having attended Lutheran schools (preschool through 12th grade), I imagined that after receiving my teaching certificates, I would develop an inclusive special education program at a local Lutheran school. For a time, my plan and what I believed to be God's plan seemed to be in agreement. Just before it was time to student teach, I received a part-time teaching position as a resource specialist with Lutheran Special Education Ministries (LSEM). My student teaching experience afforded me the flexibility to work mornings for LSEM and complete my clinical practice in the afternoons at a public school. To me this was a sign that God was clearing obstacles and leading me to follow the path of Lutheran teaching. However, over the course of a semester, a variety of people spoke into my heart and mind, leading me to live out my vocation in public school. It has been nearly 25 years since God impressed upon my heart the vocation of teaching. He has been with me throughout my career, providing opportunities to cultivate my knowledge and apply my skills in a variety of ways. Today, as I write this reflection, I know that God is working in, with, and through me. I am learning to trust that by His grace and guidance His purpose for my life will be fulfilled according to His will, not mine. I am grateful that God led me into public education, and I am grateful that I can support future educators (public and private) who are led to Concordia University Irvine. To me, vocation is a verb—a living, breathing, changing action that I actively pursue every day.

Why Teaching?

The authors provided a glimpse into personal reasons for entering the field of education. Research has identified many reasons why people choose teaching as a career path. Two studies help to answer the question, "Why teaching?" Information on what motivates people to choose a teaching path, as well as characteristics of teachers who strive to be agents of change in the field, provide some answers to this question.

Findings from a 2012 international study conducted by Watt et al. revealed that opportune samples from Australia, the United States, Germany, and Norway rated intrinsic value, perceived teaching ability, social contribution, desire to work with children/adolescents, and prior experience with positive teaching and learning as key motivation factors for why people choose the teaching profession. These findings challenge the long-held belief that people enter the field of education for reasons of job and financial security. Watt et al.'s (2012) study focused on the motivational factors for teaching; however, one recommendation for the future suggested an exploration to determine if certain personality types were more drawn to the profession.

While exploring the characteristics of teachers as change agents, van der Heijden et al. (2015) reported that the most significant characteristics attributed to teachers by teachers, principals, and external experts included "lifelong learning (being eager to learn and reflective), mastery (giving guidance, being accessible, positive, committed, trustful, and self-assured), entrepreneurship (being innovative and feeling responsible), and collaboration (being collegial)" (p. 681). The study concluded that these four primary characteristics are closely related and reinforce one another. Therefore, teachers who strive to provide excellent learning opportunities to their students take the initiative to pursue continued development and share their knowledge with their colleagues through collaboration. While individual teachers may feel that certain of these characteristics resonate more than others, it is likely they can find themselves nodding in agreement with many of them.

Teachers as Lifelong Learners

One important, research-based characteristic for teachers is an openness to lifelong learning. Continuing education is common in many fields, and education is no different. Teachers are expected to participate in professional development to expand their knowledge base, strike a balance between digital and life skills, and to foster resourcefulness and creativity (Cortezano et al., 2021). In education, the phrase "lifelong learner" assumes that educators are self-motivated to pursue professional knowledge formally and informally for their careers. After all, who wants the members of their community, let alone their child, to be taught by someone whose knowledge and practices are antiquated? How an educator engages in learning is often flexible and may depend on the internal motivation and external forces occurring at any given moment.

After completing the basic formal training to become a teacher, one may pursue additional education opportunities. This path may lead to certificates, authorizations, or advanced degrees. Formal learning settings are usually structured and facilitated by an instructor who determines what and often how learning will occur. Another path is to pursue informal training, such as attending professional seminars. In this type of learning setting, educators may select what they would like to focus on learning. Another informal type of learning is joining professional learning communities or communities of practice. Here, the decisions about what will be learned and how learning will occur can be collective. This path has the potential to offer educators supportive networks of professionals with whom they can brainstorm, strategize, and glean support. A final popular option for professional development is self-directed learning. This path is the most independent and allows the educator to self-select all aspects of the learning. Common self-directed learning options include reading books and articles relevant to a topic of interest, watching videos, listening to podcasts, or exploring reliable websites.

Regardless of the chosen path, it is important for educators to be wise, honorable, and cultivated. Well-informed educators rely on obtaining knowledge from a variety of reliable sources. Christian teachers understand that the Bible is the ultimate foundation for truth and the source of direction regarding all aspects of life, including vocations in public and Christian sectors. Teachers must be cognizant of the difference between shifting sands and solid foundations in order to stay true and authentic no matter the working environment.

Connections to Vocation

Teaching is a vocation no matter the school, grade level, student population, or level of teaching experience. A biblical stance regarding the use of authority for the good of others is a starting place for discussing a vocational mindset toward the field. All children are precious and miraculous, fearfully and wonderfully made (Psalm 139:14), and this truth should inform any teacher working to serve and impart knowledge to someone in their care. How each of us deals with the inevitable ethical dilemmas can also reflect a vocational approach. It is in the challenging as well as the exciting moments that teachers work to build up the body of Christ and/or work for the welfare of the world as displayed in their classroom and school communities (Ephesians 4:12; Jeremiah 29:7). Mackie (2017) described it this way: when you see a human working, you are seeing the image of God.

It is important to note that working conditions and environments range from boldly Christian to hostile toward Christian values. Loy (2020) provides a reminder that a vocational mindset does not mean removing oneself from spaces shared in common with unbelievers. Working already contains a spiritual dimension (Veith, 2011), and schools represent communities where opportunities to serve others abound. For teachers, this service might take the form of tying a shoe, correcting a behavior, or explaining a concept in a new way. Yes, it might also be answering a student asking why you mention going to church every time you share about your weekend. Vocation is not specific to certain church-related careers or roles; it encompasses any role where gifts are used to serve others (Wingren, 1942/2004). Martin Luther insisted on this broader understanding of vocation as opposed to a more narrow definition that only included work done in the church (Maas, 2015). A teacher with a vocational mindset approaches everything about the role as spiritually significant, where even the most mundane is meaningful.

Conclusion

The field of education will never be void of controversy, challenges, and the effects of a changing cultural worldview. However, strength comes from understanding teaching as a calling from God, sanctified by Christ, and firmly anchored in biblical truth. Viewing teaching as a vocation applies no matter the school or the learning environment. Each teacher will have a unique professional journey, individual experiences, and ongoing learning opportunities, but a vocational lens highlights one aspect all teachers have in common: the opportunity to use gifts and talents to serve others.

References

Bandura, A. (1982). Self-efficacy mechanism in human agency. *American psychologist*, *37*(2), 122. https://doi.org/10.1037/0003-066X.37.2.122

Cortezano, G. P., Maningas, R. V., Yazon, A. D., Buenvinida, L. P., Tan, C. S., & Tamban, V. E. (2021). Lived experiences of educators engaged in continuing professional development in the new normal: Insights from seven countries. *International Journal of Management, Entrepreneurship, Social Science and Humanities*, *4*(2), 129–45. https://researchsynergy.org/ijmesh/

Darling-Hammond, L., & Hyler, M. E. (2020). Preparing educators for the time of COVID and beyond. *European Journal of Teacher Education*, *43*(4), 457–65. https://doi.org/10.1080/02619768.2020.1816961

EAB. (2023a). Building a better behavior management strategy for students and teachers: Key findings from EAB's student behavior survey. Education Advisory Board. https://pages.eab.com/StudentBehaviorSurveyExecutiveBriefSuccess.html

EAB. (2023b). *2023 voice of the superintendent: Key survey findings and critical conversations for the year ahead*. Education Advisory Board. https://pages.eab.com/2023SuperintendentSurveyExecutiveBrief.html

Heyward, G. (2021, September 17). TikTok's latest craze: Stealing stuff from school. *The New York Times*. https://www.nytimes.com/2021/09/17/us/devious-licks-tiktok.html

Hill, C. E. (2020). *Motivation to teach: The influence of self-efficacy and job satisfaction on teacher retention in an urban California school system* [Doctoral dissertation, Concordia University Irvine]. Concordia Digital Repository. http://hdl.handle.net/11414/3460

Kelly, M. (2021, December 9). *Political polarization and its echo chambers: Surprising new, cross-disciplinary perspectives from Princeton*. Princeton University. https://www.princeton.edu/news/2021/12/09/political-polarization-and-its-echo-chambers-surprising-new-cross-disciplinary

Loy, D. W. (2020). Confessions of a Lutheran university. *Concordia Theological Journal*, *7*(1), 60–76. https://www.cuw.edu/academics/schools/arts-and-sciences/_assets/theological-journal/2020_v7i1-Winter/Article3-Loy.pdf

Maas, K. D. (2015). The vocation of a student. In S. A. Ashmon (Ed.), *The idea and practice of a Christian university: A Lutheran approach* (pp. 91–114). Concordia Publishing House.

Mackie, T. (Host). (2017, August 30). *Theology of work: A story about work* [Audio podcast]. Bible Project. https://bibleproject.com/podcast/theology-work-part-1-story-about-work/

Richtel, M. (2022, April 23). "It's life or death": The mental health crisis among US teens. *The New York Times.* https://www.nytimes.com/2022/04/23/health/mental-health-crisis-teens.html

Saloviita, T., & Pakarinen, E. (2021). Teacher burnout explained: Teacher-, student-, and organisation-level variables. *Teaching and Teacher Education*, *97*. https://doi.org/10.1016/j.tate.2020.103221

van der Heijden, H. R. M. A., Geldens, J. J. M., Beijaard, D., & Popeijus, H. L. (2015). Characteristics of teachers as change agents. *Teachers and Teaching*, *21*(6), 681–99. https://doi.org/10.1080/13540602.2015.1044328

Veith, G. E. (2011). Vocation: The theology of the Christian life. *Journal of Markets & Morality*, *14*(1). https://www.marketsandmorality.com/index.php/mandm/article/view/14

Watt, H. M. G., Richardson, P. W., Klusmann, U., Kunter, M., Beyer, B., Trautwein, U., & Baumert, J. (2012). Motivations for choosing teaching as a career: An international comparison using the FIT-Choice scale. *Teaching and Teacher Education*, *28*(6), 791–805. https://doi.org/10.1016/j.tate.2012.03.003

Wingren, G. (2004). *Luther on vocation* (C. C. Rasmussen, Trans.). Wipf & Stock. (Original work published 1942)

Ziaian-Ghafari, N., & Berg, D. H. (2019). Compassion fatigue: The experiences of teachers working with students with exceptionalities. *Exceptionality Education International*, *29*(1), 32–53. https://eric.ed.gov/?id=EJ1212170

A VOCATION OF SERVICE: HEALTHCARE ADMINISTRATION

Curt Gielow

Curt Gielow, PharmB, MHA, was the founding Dean of the Concordia University Wisconsin School of Pharmacy. He was awarded an honorary doctorate from Concordia University Ann Arbor in Michigan for his service and leadership in the revitalization of that university campus. He has also served as a Wisconsin State Representative and Mayor of the city of Mequon.

Career advice comes easy, but *good* career advice is hard to find. Some business books written to assist the reader in identifying and finding a good job focus only on the tangible aspects of the position. If the more tangible benefits are all you care about, then it may be relatively easy to find a job. However, finding a job that matches your perceived talents with an opportunity that forecasts good pay, high demand, and a good long-term future can be difficult.

There is an old adage suggesting that if you truly enjoy your job, then it is not really work. Enjoying your job or work is hopefully about matching your passion with an occupation that fulfills your innate desire to be useful and helpful to others. *Finding your God-given talents is the challenge.* Today careers in healthcare have drawn significant attention. Such careers, either in direct patient care or administration, draw interest from individuals who have identified their passion to help others. In the times of Martin Luther, the word "vocation" referred to the call by God to an individual primarily to the priesthood or the religious life. Luther expanded the understanding of vocation or divine callings to include most secular occupations and other roles in ordinary life.

Gene Edward Veith, in *Working for Our Neighbor*, says, "For Martin Luther, vocation is nothing less than the locus of the Christian life. God works in and through vocation, but he does so by calling human beings to work in their vocations."[1] Veith further writes, "According to Luther's doctrine of vocation, the purpose of every vocation is to love and serve our neighbors."[2]

Healthcare Administration

Simply defined, healthcare administration is the practice of administering, leading, overseeing, and managing the complex and dynamic business entities that include physician practices, hospitals, clinics, long-term care facilities, pharmacies, and health insurance providers. The administrators of these entities are the operational leaders who guide these organizations through organizational efficiency, growth, and change. *These are servant-leaders practicing the vocation of healthcare administration.*

In my experience individuals drawn to the profession of healthcare administration will be challenged to display certain skills and aptitudes. I'll mention a few that may be obvious to the seasoned management executive but nevertheless are important to this exploration of healthcare management as a vocation.

The vocation of healthcare administration deals frequently with ethical dilemmas involving physicians, patients and their families, other care providers, pharmaceutical use, and medical equipment. If Christians truly live their beliefs and faith, then they should have the integrity to lead others in a management role by example. We should all be seen as Christians because of how we are seen as individuals. An example of my personal experience challenging my integrity is set forth later in this chapter. My experience has been that your integrity—your honest, candid, and professional words and actions—define you as a servant-leader and are absolutely key to being a successful leader in the complex vocation of healthcare administration.

The ability to manage relationships, personal and professional, is a skill absolutely required to be effective in dealing with the complex and varied audiences requiring a healthcare administrator's attention.

1 Gene Edward Veith, *Working for Our Neighbor: A Lutheran Primer on Vocation, Economics, and Ordinary Life* (Grand Rapids, MI: Christian's Library Press, 2016), 13.

2 Veith, *Working for Our Neighbor*, 13.

The range of relationships from physicians, caregivers of many kinds, patients and their families, the community, the government, and healthcare payers, just to name some, will challenge even the best executive. Developing good working relationships with key caregivers, especially colleagues, in the delivery of healthcare services is a must. Leaders lead by example as much as any other way. Christian leaders, committed to the vocation of care for others, which Luther defines as love, should develop relationships with colleagues that ensure the fulfillment of the mission of the ministry or business in which they work. Effective leaders who master relationships for the betterment of the organization do so because they understand communication—immediate, honest, and effective communication between all layers of an organization.

Like many businesses, healthcare is undergoing significant and convulsive change. The industry is struggling with increasing costs, new technologies that should (but don't seem to) lower cost, and ethical issues around life and death and whose rights are to be honored in those decisions. The current healthcare delivery mechanism, called Direct Primary Care, is attempting to return power to the patient and the physician and away from big insurance companies. There is ongoing debate about whether the creation of large healthcare organizations where multiple hospitals and their affiliated clinics and physicians merge together is helping our healthcare delivery or simply increasing already high costs. The continuing mergers of ever larger healthcare organizations seem to sometimes stress the original mission of the smaller original organizations. The articulation of an organization's mission and values is a critically important skill to be honed by an effective leader. Strategic plans are no longer long-view forecasts looking into the future five years out. Rather they should integrate the values of the organization with the mission of the organization. Key performance indicators specific to achieving the mission in accordance with the organization's values and objectives are the guide posts for staying on track. All of this challenges the healthcare leader to be effective in communications, change management, and relationship development.

Equally important to good leaders is an acute awareness and sensitivity to the fundamental fact that we are called to care for all people whom God created and to work effectively with them. Healthcare executives are essentially responsible for the effective delivery of healthcare services to people of diverse backgrounds and ethnicities. Cultural or economic barriers to quality care for all people must be understood and eliminated with a zeal for inclusiveness that this vocation demands. This awareness of diversity and inclusion is a bedrock tenet of Christian love. John recounts in Revelation 7:9, "After this I looked, and behold, a great multitude that no one could number, from every nation, from all tribes and peoples and languages, standing before the throne and before the Lamb, clothed in white robes, with palm branches in their hands." This is simply a reminder that God's people need to care for *every person God created* with the vocational love Luther espoused.

Personal Stories

To highlight several of the required skills and personality traits I have put forth in this chapter, I offer these examples.

I started to follow my vocational interest in a career in healthcare at the University of Illinois in the 1960s. I choose premed as my initial goal. However, I struggled mightily with the anatomy and physiology classes, yet did well in chemistry. I had two roommates who were both studying prepharmacy at the time. I did so poorly in parts of the premed curriculum that I considered a switch to pharmacy, largely influenced by the late-night discussions with these roommates.

After my first tumultuous college year at the U of I, I decided to try pharmacy. I felt my vocation was in service to others, and I had a significant interest in becoming a healthcare provider, so I decided to try something other than premed. This revised educational plan required me to raise my GPA as the first order of business if I was to get a serious look from any college of pharmacy in the country. I enrolled in a local community college near my hometown to focus on getting the required prerequisite courses and to get my GPA up. Mission accomplished in 12 months, and I entered pharmacy school as a third-year student and successfully graduated several years later.

I landed a wonderful position as the chief pharmacist (really the only pharmacist) in a small Catholic-sponsored hospital in southern Illinois. I commenced to implement innovations in pharmacy care, adopted new technologies, and offered enhanced services and any other innovative ideas I could conceive and implement. During this early period of establishing my vocation as a servant-leader I encountered my first ethical crisis. I discovered that a pharmacy assistant, working as a pharmacy department intern, was abetting his sister, a nurse at the hospital, in falsifying the daily narcotic record of the number/amount of narcotic drug ampules used for the patients on the nursing floor. When the accounting of the pharmacy-supplied narcotics appeared not to match the patient prescribed narcotics record kept by the nurses, an investigation was commenced. We found the nurse (his sister) had developed a narcotic habit to treat her own severe back pain, and her brother (my intern) knew it. She was using a dose each day and falsifying the record to indicate a patient had received that ampule via injection. When confronted, my intern begged me to forgive him and go as easy as possible on his sister. Although I believe, as many do, that people deserve second chances, two wrongs don't make a right.

Although I agonized over the decision, I fired the young man and recommended the same fate for his nurse sister. The hospital did not pursue any legal actions against either of them. My dismissal of the young man was done with as much Christian charity and compassion as possible, with more of a lesson-learned approach than with severe chastisement. I periodically reflect on what became of the young man trying to help his hurting sister. Did my treatment of him become a life lesson that helped him move on to a successful occupation outside of pharmacy? I do believe in second chances, but when they cannot be offered, as in this case, the method and treatment of punishment of the guilty is required to be proportional so as to not create permanent scars. I believe my handling of this situation fit the doctrine of Luther's focus on vocation being about love while challenging my empathy and integrity.

In a second example of the skills necessary for the vocation of healthcare administration, I was asked later in my career to step into a failing hospital enterprise and try to revive it to keep this small hospital operating in a specific inner-city location where healthcare services were sparse. The hospital had only a few physicians using the services and fewer than ten patients in the average daily census. Losing money, unable to afford necessary personnel and losing the support and confidence of physicians—this was a difficult business turnaround challenge and one with slim chances of survival. Nevertheless, several things needed to be done and done quickly. In relating my actions, I highlight several key skill sets I believe make a good leader.

Communication: I called an all-employee meeting of the day- and evening-shift personnel, and a separate meeting of all night-shift personnel, to tell everybody how bad the situation of survival for this hospital was. My integrity required a full and honest assessment of the situation.

Relationship Management: I met collectively and then individually with the physicians who used this hospital and begged them to remain loyal and admit their patients to our hospital while pledging to them our continued commitment to quality patient care. I told them I would keep them apprised of the business circumstances each week.

Strategic Thinking: How in the world were we going to turn around a failing business in the quickest possible timeframe? I met daily with the senior management of the hospital and the department heads to convey the current circumstances, most frequently about cash flow issues necessary to meet payroll needs, let alone to pay vendors for necessary supplies. This required a short-term strategic plan to maximize the use of every dollar so that only essentials were paid, debt was negotiated to be in forbearance, and efforts were redoubled to collect outstanding accounts receivables from individuals, the state, and federal government programs.

Business Acumen and Change Management: This turnaround project was the toughest business challenge I had ever faced at the time. It required many people to agree to participate for the greater good. Keeping a professional clinical staff under these circumstances was difficult, as all the nurses could go anywhere else for employment if they had even a hint that we could not save this hospital from closing. To their credit, largely because we effectively communicated with honesty and candor, most stayed in their jobs.

Empathy: After some, but inconsistent, signs of improving business circumstances, we lost the confidence of the local bank. They refused to issue more credit despite our marginally improving financial condition. Finally, after a last-ditch effort was made in a personal meeting with the key bank officers, they pulled the plug and demanded immediate repayment of all debt. This, of course, was not possible, and their action therefore necessitated placing the hospital in bankruptcy. That day we laid off more than 100 wonderful people who not only lost their jobs but their pension and any benefits too. Although I don't think anyone blamed me for laying them off, it was a terrible day!

These examples illustrate the passion I had for my calling to the vocation of healthcare administration. But as the personal stories also show, the outcome is not always what we want in our work. The Lord tells us that in this world we will have troubles. As He said in John 16:33, "In the world you will have tribulation. But take heart; I have overcome the world."

Finding an occupation that feels like a calling, like God's call to a vocation, is not always easy and obvious. Whatever occupation you choose, pursue it with passion and a sincere commitment to make a difference. Be significant to somebody or something. We should be able to tell anyone *why* we do what we do. The *why* is important. Our *why* shapes how we approach each and every day and at times each moment and person. The *why* of where we are also shapes *what* that we are doing, and both the *why* and the *what* combined tell others *who* we are, and should also show *whose* we are too. We should all have a *why* to our *what* that shapes *who* we are. This holds true whether we practice in a large healthcare organization or a small, personalized healthcare setting like the Direct Primary Care medical practices that are now growing all around the country. *Where* you provide your service to the Lord is usually determined by the professional opportunities that present themselves or the individual choices you make in your career. This is the calling that requires discernment of *why*, *what*, *when*, and *where*. Our

Lord just wants us to care for and love one another and use the gifts He has given us—Luther's clear understanding of vocation.

In his rendition of the Bible, called *The Message*, Eugene Peterson paraphrased Ephesians 1:11–12 like so: "It's in Christ that we find out who we are and what we are living for. Long before we first heard of Christ . . . , he had his eye on us, had designs on us for glorious living, part of the overall purpose he is working out in everything and everyone" (MSG).

The healthcare industry holds many opportunities to find an occupation that fits the skills, talents, and interests God has given you. If you want to serve others in a vocation of love as defined by Luther, you have many options. Not everything will go right every day, and some days will test your faith in the choices you make. But choices can be changed. My experiences as a college freshman redirected my focus from premed to pharmacy. A few years of pharmacy practice changed my focus once again to healthcare administration when my boss gave me assignments beyond pharmacy responsibilities that opened my eyes to the potential to serve in an alternative way. For the last 15 years of my working life, my healthcare experiences were refocused to a new vocation in higher education at Concordia University Wisconsin, where I used all of my previous healthcare experiences to become a founding Dean of a new pharmacy school at the university. Later I also served six years leading a reinvigoration and strategic focusing effort toward healthcare academic program development at the Concordia University campus in Ann Arbor, Michigan. That business challenge required all the skills and experiences of a combined 40 years of healthcare management. Colleges aren't unlike hospitals. Recognizing new opportunities that the Lord presents for us today, albeit different from those of the past but yet all part of His plan for us, is a simulating and energizing experience. I believe God presents these opportunities as chapters in our life of service to Him. I've had at least seven chapters in my vocational life of service. I pray I have pleased the Lord with my contributions in healthcare, higher education, and community service.

The apostle Paul points out the significant pleasure God had in the service of His servant David: "David . . . served the purpose of God in his own generation" (Acts 13:36). Rick Warren suggests that this is the greatest epitaph one could receive.[3] We should all try to serve God's purpose in our generation.

3 Rick Warren, *The Purpose Driven Life: What on Earth Am I Here For?* (Grand Rapids, MI: Zondervan, 2002), 318.

SERVING GOD IN PUBLIC HEALTH PROFESSIONS

Jennifer Janousek

Dr. Jennifer Janousek is Professor of Health and Human Performance at Concordia University Nebraska. She teaches at the graduate and undergraduate levels, and she directed the Master of Public Health Program from 2010 to 2019. Janousek is a Certified Health Education Specialist (CHES) and volunteers with public health efforts at both the local and state level. She was the Chair of the Public Health Education Section and Board Member for the Public Health Association of Nebraska for many years and was named Health Teacher of the Year by SHAPE (Society of Health & Physical Educators) Nebraska in 2017.

> Now there are varieties of gifts, but the same Spirit; and there are varieties of service, but the same Lord; and there are varieties of activities, but it is the same God who empowers them all in everyone.
>
> *1 Corinthians 12:4–6*

Before really understanding vocation, I used to simply relate it to my future or current occupation. Vocation, in my mind, did not necessarily relate to my role outside of my public health professional life. In my own faith development over the years and in researching the concept of vocation, I have come to better understand vocation and what it means. I appreciate Gene Edward Veith's observation that vocation means calling, but "calling" does not necessarily mean hearing God's voice beckoning you to do some great work for Him (Veith, 2007). It is very easy to misinterpret the word "calling" and associate it with God specifically telling you to do some particular task. Vocation includes our everyday activities through which God can and does work. Vocation includes not only what we are called to do but also what God does through our callings.

It is easy to associate vocation with the works that you are supposed to do. I love the saying taken from Luther that we are "masks of God" in our vocations (Veith, 2016, p. 3). Selfishly, I sometimes think of vocation as something that I do and not necessarily as something that God does. God works through all things, and all good comes from God. I cannot take credit for any good work or deed but rather praise God for working through all things in both my personal and professional life to share His love and grace in service to others. This is a constant reminder that I need on a daily basis. I also am guilty of being quick to thank humans but slow to recognize that God was the one working through them.

Before diving into public health as a vocation, let us first define public health. Although not termed "public health" then, public health has essentially been around since the earliest times. The book of Leviticus contains one of the first codes of health laws, including food regulations to protect the health of people and laws for quarantine to prevent plagues. According to the American Public Health Association, "Public health promotes and protects the health of people and their communities. This science-based, evidence-backed field strives to give everyone a safe place to live, learn, work and play" (2023). Healthcare treats individuals and families who are sick, but public health works to prevent people from getting sick in the first place by preventing diseases and improving the health of populations by promoting healthy lifestyles. Public health professionals administer educational programs, develop and recommend policies, administer services, and conduct research. Public health work also involves promoting healthcare equity, quality, and accessibility. The three widely recognized core functions of public health are assessment, policy development, and assurance. The profession recognizes the 10 Essential Public Health Services, created by a task force of public health experts and promoted by the Center for Disease Control, which describe the public health activities that should be effectively delivered in all communities (see figure 1).

At the center of the core functions and 10 essential services is equity. Public health entities need to consider how the conditions in the places where people live, learn, work, play, and worship affect a wide range of health risks and outcomes. These social determinants of health are nonmedical factors that influence health outcomes; they include education access and quality, economic stability, healthcare access and quality, neighborhood and built environment (e.g., safe housing, transportation, access to nutritious food, polluted air and water), and social and community context (racism, discrimination, and violence) (US Department of Health and Human Services, 2023). Actions to address the resulting health inequities should be incorporated throughout all aspects of public health work.

Today, public health professionals work in a variety of settings, including the public, private, academic, and nonprofit sectors. Common work environments include health departments, state and federal agencies (such as public safety and environmental agencies), community-based organizations (including human service, charity, and education/youth development organizations), hospitals, private consulting firms, corporate businesses, and international organizations. However, this list is certainly not comprehensive, as public health professionals may work for a wide variety of employers in various settings. An incredibly diverse number of occupations fall under the public health umbrella, as it is a very broad, all-encompassing field. In fact, it is difficult to think of any field that is not involved in public health. The arts and humanities are frequently used therapeutically to improve health. Engineering must be involved in designing buildings for disaster mitigation and proper ventilation, a major responsibility of public health. All of the sciences are utilized in disease treatment and prevention, and economic entities and governmental positions are vital to keeping community, state, national, and global health systems operating.

Lutheran theology teaches that each Christian has multiple vocations that exist in four estates: the church, the household, society, and the workplace.[1] I believe that our work in public health could be located in all four estates. According to the Lutheran understanding, the purpose of public health vocations is to love and serve our neighbors using

1 Luther identified three estates; he included family life and economic activity in the single estate of *oeconomia*. With the advent of the industrial revolution, economic activity moved out of the home, leading more recent theologians to identify four estates.

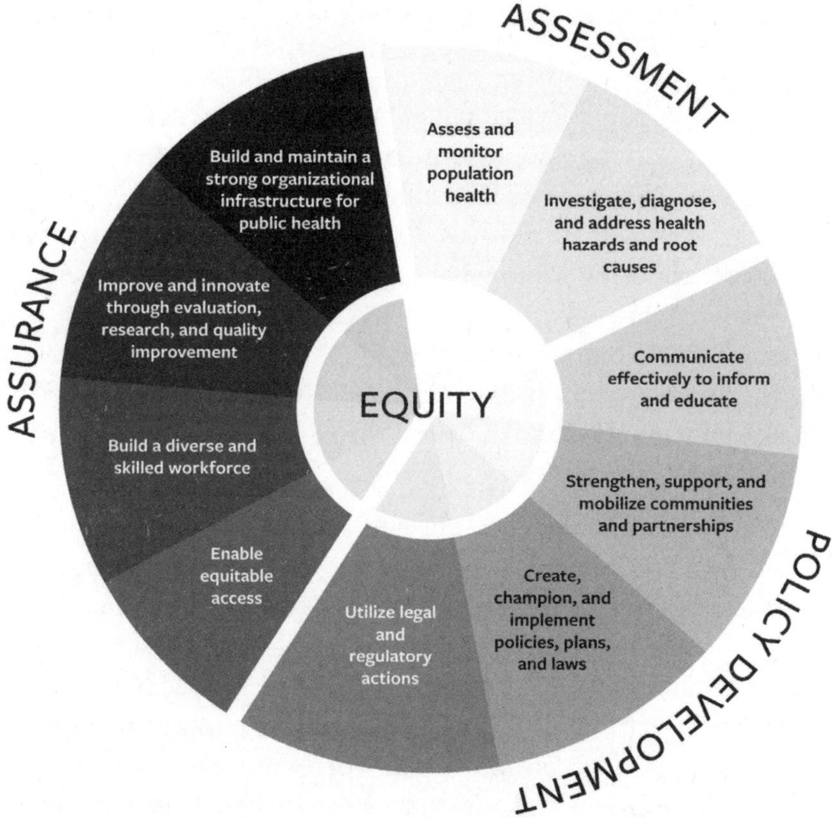

Figure 1. The 10 Essential Public Health Services.

10 Essential Public Health Services Futures Initiative Task Force. (2020, September 9). 10 essential public health services. https://phaboard.org/center-for-innovation/public-health-frameworks/the-10-essential-public-health-services/

our specific professional training. We can do this in the church through parish health and health education programs, affordable housing development, and food pantries; in our homes as we love our families and teach them to care for their bodies through good nutrition and healthy lifestyle choices; in society by improving the health of others through education and political activism; and in the workplace in a variety of ways depending on our specific public health career.

Whatever you do, work heartily, as for the Lord and not for men.
Colossians 3:23

Our work in public health could be considered a holy order in that we are simply serving people and trying to help them enjoy a higher quality of life. This servant-leadership should be done out of sincere love rather than selfish motives. To me this means working with a happy heart, choosing to do what is best for my neighbor even if that means harder work for me, and always putting others before myself (Colossians 3:23; Mark 12:31; Acts 20:35). Luther wrote, "We conclude, therefore, that a Christian lives not in himself, but in Christ and in his neighbor. . . . He lives in Christ through faith, and in his neighbor through love" (*Luther's Works* 31:371).

God's Word provides wisdom and insight into the public health field and into those we are called to serve. There is a close connection between public health and the biblical theme of compassion and helping all in need despite their circumstances (e.g., Matthew 9:12–13; John 5:1–9; Luke 10:25–37; 1 Peter 3:8–9). In the public health field, we work with people from all walks of life, which requires us to engage in a sinful world. In this vocation, we will work with people who may have different belief systems and may make lifestyle choices we do not agree with. You do not have to agree with someone's lifestyle to show care and compassion and to help that person improve his or her health. Jesus teaches us not to judge others (Matthew 7:1–2), and the Bible repeatedly tells us the importance of loving others (1 Corinthians 13:1–6, 13; 16:14). Jesus showed mercy to people caught in sin throughout the New Testament (Mark 6:34; John 4; 8:4–11). Jesus set the perfect example for us of not condoning sin but also not condemning the sinner. Our professional work in public health regularly brings us side by side with nonbelievers. We may not always have the opportunity to share biblical truths with those with whom we work, but we have the amazing opportunity to show them God's love and compassion as we help them avoid diseases and improve their health, and we have the chance to pray for them to come to the Lord and "come to the knowledge of the truth" (1 Timothy 2:4).

God works through public health to bless others and brings public health practitioners into diverse, underserved communities. In other words, our work as public health professionals is an important part of God's left-hand kingdom, in which God uses us human beings to help one another flourish in our lives.[2] What an amazing opportunity to influence the world outside of ourselves and outside of our own neighborhoods! In public health, we work with vulnerable populations including the economically disadvantaged, racial and ethnic minorities, the disabled, the homeless, the elderly, the uninsured, low-income children, rural residents, those with human immunodeficiency virus (HIV), and those with other chronic conditions including mental health challenges. The vulnerabilities of these individuals are exacerbated by race, ethnicity, age, sex, and the social determinants of health. We can bless these vulnerable individuals by helping to meet their needs as masks of God through whom He "richly and daily provides" everything they need "to support this body and life" (Small Catechism, Creed, First Article). As public health professionals, we have a unique opportunity to bring community partners, including churches and Christian organizations, together at the same table to solve complex health challenges, to link people to services, and to strive for health equity for all whom God created and for whom Christ died and rose.

Even though we can always treat people with the same love and compassion that Jesus did, we also have the opportunity to choose jobs within the field that are aligned with our faith. We have our personal views, our Christian views, and our professional views. It is nice when they align, but that is not always the case. There may be some positions or organizations that you choose not to apply to or work for because of conflict with your Christian beliefs—public health organizations that condone lifestyles not in alignment with God's Word or positions that require advocating for reproductive rights that you may disagree with. Just as in other vocations, there will be moral dilemmas and ethical challenges that will require you to use discernment.

Consider this ethical dilemma. You are working as a public health

2 See David W. Loy's essay "Vocation, Work, and Human Flourishing" in this volume for a discussion of the doctrine of the two kingdoms.

educator for a local health department and have been assigned to work with a family in your community whose 12-year-old daughter is pregnant. You are tasked with educating and linking this family with services and resources to help the daughter and her new baby. You have the immense opportunity to look out for the well-being of the daughter and to provide a supportive, caring presence as you address challenges she will face with continuing her education and caring for herself and her new baby. As you talk with her about issues related to sexual education and safe sex, you stress the importance of abstinence and refraining from sexual relations until she is married. Knowing her personal history, do you encourage the girl's mother to put the 12-year-old on birth control after the birth of her baby, even though you have strong religious beliefs against premarital sex and know the girl is too young emotionally and physically to have sex? You have read the research, and you know that the likelihood of her abstaining from future sexual activity after already initiating the behavior at such a young age is low, but you also do not want to condone sexual activity by encouraging the girl to use birth control. However, it is in everyone's best interest to prevent a subsequent pregnancy. Perhaps the best approach is to share health information and not our opinions and beliefs.

Another dilemma to consider. You are pro-life and disagree with abortion services being included with "reproductive health rights" as a public health issue. A national professional association is a strong advocate for abortion rights you strongly oppose. However, the organization also advocates for many other health initiatives not related to abortion that you do agree with, and you gain many educational and networking benefits by being a member of the organization and attending its conferences. Should an individual not support an organization through membership dues and conference attendance if the organization's mission is not entirely aligned with the individual's beliefs? On one hand, those membership fees and conference fees would indirectly provide financial support for the organization's continued fight to protect access and rights to abortion. On the other hand, those funds would also give a professional member the opportunity to learn about the latest research, best practices, and advocacy strategies for improving health outcomes, and membership would provide networking opportunities with other public health experts in the field.

These are difficult dilemmas. Uncertainty is common with complicated ethical issues. Christians with similar beliefs may come to different conclusions. Each of us must choose the best answer he or she can with the information available. These are just two of many quandaries you may encounter as a public health professional. Some of the dilemmas you will come across in your professional public health career will not involve conflicts with the Christian faith but rather deep disagreements about moral and political principles in the left-hand kingdom. These dilemmas may involve the distribution of healthcare (is healthcare a right or a privilege?); paternalistic interventions versus respect for autonomous choices and liberties; distributive justice; balancing individual and public interests; screening, testing, and contact tracing; voluntary versus mandatory immunization programs; and containing communicable diseases through involuntary quarantines (as in the case of individuals with tuberculosis or measles, and more recently with stay-at-home orders and quarantines for the COVID-19 pandemic), just to name a few.

> Truly, I say to you, as you did it to one of the least of these My brothers, you did it to Me.
>
> *Matthew 25:40*

The Public Health Code of Ethics is a set of professional standards and expectations for public health practitioners. It was originally developed in 2002 by the Public Health Leadership Society. In 2019, the American Public Health Association published an updated version of these ethical standards and obligations to guide decision-making for both practitioners and institutions. You may find these public health core values and obligations helpful when working in the field:

1. ***Professionalism and Trust.*** Keep promises and commitments. Use evidence-based decision-making and an ethical framework in decision-making. Maintain transparency and honesty by disclosing conflicts of interest.

2. ***Health and Safety.*** Prevent or minimize harm, and "promote and protect the public's safety, health, and well-being."
3. ***Health Justice and Equity.*** Seek equal opportunities for the realization of health by all, regardless of gender, ethnic, social, economic, or geographic status.
4. ***Interdependence and Solidarity.*** Each person's health is tied to the health of the community, and we all share the burden of promoting and maintaining health.
5. ***Human Rights and Civil Liberties.*** All humans deserve protection of life, health, and well-being. All humans deserve protection from harm as well as respect for autonomous choice and actions, while also protecting privacy and confidentiality.
6. ***Inclusivity and Engagement.*** Be transparent and accountable, and ensure diverse public participation. (American Public Health Association, 2019)

There are points in the Public Health Code of Ethics that are consistent with tenets of the Christian faith. For example, in point 1, there is an obvious tie to Christian faith in terms of being trustworthy and honest (Proverbs 12:22; 2 Corinthians 8:21; Colossians 3:9). Point 2, about protecting the health, safety, and well-being of others, is reminiscent of Matthew 25:40–45. Point 3, despite the politically loaded language, certainly seems to reflect God's admonition for us to love all our neighbors, and it fits with Christ's willingness to heal even Gentiles (John 13:34; 1 Peter 4:8; Galatians 5:13). Point 5, while again couched in the language of modern political theory, still reflects a notion of human dignity that can be found in Scripture, even if it does not perfectly overlap with Scripture (Genesis 1:26–27; Matthew 10:24; Luke 6:36). Christians can often find points of contact between the secular moral codes of their professions and the scriptural view of humanity and God's love for us in Christ.

> Do nothing from selfish ambition or conceit, but in humility count others more significant than yourselves. Let each of you look not only to his own interests, but also to the interests of others.
>
> *Philippians 2:3–4*

In the field of public health, our work obviously addresses the needs and interests of others as we improve the health of populations, but it also addresses our own self-interest to provide financially for ourselves and our families. With any profession, including public health, it is easy to get caught up with personal pieties, spiritualities, or glories that do not actually serve our neighbor. Veith (2016) points out that "*every vocation* has its moral temptations, struggles of conscience, and points of tension with the Christian faith" (p. 61). We all sin in our public health vocations and sin against our public health vocations. For example, we may ask ourselves, "How can I gain from this profession? Or how can I increase my salary? How many times can I get published?" If I am working and completing certain tasks simply to benefit myself, I am only serving myself and not others. The problem is not seeking satisfaction in the profession or pursuing a higher salary or trying publish. The problem is viewing the profession merely as an opportunity to serve ourselves rather than a means of serving others. Our work will still benefit others as God continues to work through us in this calling, but our attitudes put us in danger of viewing the people we are serving simply as means for achieving our own ends. These conflicts become opportunities to exercise our faith by repenting of selfish attitudes and seeking Christ's forgiveness. They can contribute to our spiritual growth and sanctification as we learn to trust that God will provide for us or that He shows us that our service to others is the real value of what we are doing.

The doctrine of vocation brings immense dignity to all human activities that are part of sustaining and participating in human community—whether the participants know it or not. For, though "masked," God Himself is at work through our vocations and through those He has made in His image (Genesis 1:26), even in the midst of sin and a now-fallen creation. The public health field is certainly important and a source of blessing from God, but the field is not more particularly glorious or important than any other honorable occupation such as teacher, business professional, or cashier.

Our vocation, our calling, in public health is to love God and serve our fellow human beings. We can do this in many ways, shapes, and forms. There is not one specific task God tells us to do, but rather we are to love God and serve others in all that we do in our personal and professional lives. God presents us with many ways to serve, and we are free to choose more than one way to do so. There may not be a specific task we must do, but in what we choose to do, we are called to love God and serve others. God will bless others through what we choose to do.

> Whatever you do, in word or deed, do everything in the name of the Lord Jesus.
>
> *Colossians 3:17*

A special thanks to Chris and Heidi for helping me brainstorm ideas for this essay.

References

American Public Health Association. (2023). What is public health? https://www.apha.org/what-is-public-health (accessed February 26, 2024).

American Public Health Association. (2019). *Public health code of ethics*. https://www.apha.org/-/media/files/pdf/membergroups/ethics/code_of_ethics.ashx (accessed October 21, 2023).

Childress, J. F., Faden, R. R., Gaare, R. D., Gostin, L. O., Kahn, J., Bonnie, R. J., Kass, N. E., Mastroianni, A. C., Moreno, J. D., & Nieburg, P. (2002). Public health ethics: Mapping the terrain. *The Journal of Law Medicine and Ethics 30*(2), 170–78.

US Department of Health and Human Services. (2023). Social determinants of health. *Healthy People 2030*. https://health.gov/healthypeople/priority-areas/social-determinants-health

Veith, G. E. (2007, November 6). Our calling and God's glory. *Modern Reformation*. https://www.modernreformation.org/resources/articles/our-calling-and-gods-glory

Veith, G. E. (2016). *Working for our neighbor: A Lutheran primer on vocation, economics, and ordinary life.* Christian's Library Press.

COACHING AS A VOCATION

Jim Kunau

Kent Schlichtemeier

Jim Kunau, MIM, is Assistant Professor of Leadership and Director of the Master's in Coaching and Athletic Administration Program at Concordia University Irvine. Prior to coming to Concordia, Jim coached and served 21 years at Orange Lutheran High School as Athletic Director, Director of Leadership Studies, and Head Football Coach. During that time, he earned National, State, and Regional Coach of the Year honors and was named Orange County's Coach of the Decade.

Dr. Kent Schlichtemeier is Professor of Education and the inaugural Director of the Servant Leadership Institute at Concordia University Irvine. Prior to his current role at Concordia, he held numerous roles in Lutheran junior high and high schools, coached women's basketball at Concordia, and served as the Dean of the School of Education at Concordia. He was named the District Three NAIA Coach of the Year in 1992 and 1993 and was inducted into the Concordia Athletic Hall of Fame in 2006.

What Is a Vocation?

Moses was called by God at a burning bush to be a leader. He resolutely tried five times to decline this call from the Lord to lead the people of Israel from their 400-year bondage in slavery to the Egyptians. Fortunately, the Lord was ready for Moses' apprehension and was able to convince Moses that He was in this call and was going to be with him. Moses' calling in life was to transition from a life as a nomad to God's servant, willing to be used to stare down Pharaoh through ten miraculous plagues in Egypt to gain freedom for the Israelites to move to the Promised Land. Moses' vocation was clearly identified for him at the burning bush. Our callings from the Lord today are not as dramatic as what Moses experienced but can assuredly still be recognized as coming from the Lord.

Our vocation is our calling in life. Down through history God continues to work through ordinary human beings with different talents to serve Him by serving one another. This is the doctrine of vocation. God "creates and equips each person in a different way for the calling He has in mind for that person's life" (Veith, 2002, p. 21). Every kind of calling is an opportunity for serving God and one's neighbor. People with an affinity for athletics may have the opportunity to hear God's call to serve as a coach. Coaches can be what Luther describes as "masks of God" (Veith, 2002), where God's work is carried out through their lives as their actions and words touch thousands of people in society today.

Jesus, the ultimate leader, did not seek to be served but to serve. Effective coaches recognize their ultimate effectiveness comes from being a servant-leader seeking to serve their athletes above themselves. At the heart of a servant-leader's calling is the internalization and manifestation of Jesus' great commandment to love God and to love others. Spending time with Jesus on a daily basis empowers coaches to be more inclined to lead with the purpose of leaving an indelible contribution in the lives of student-athletes versus a single focus on winning athletic contests. The complex challenges that youth face in today's society, such as the high percentage of single-parent homes, social media pressures, culture wars, and moral challenges, create unprecedented responsibilities and urgency within the coaching profession to strive to impact and guide the lives of athletes for the better.

What Is a Coach?

The term "coach" originally came into the American lexicon from the days of the Old West, when stagecoaches were used to transport people from one place to another. Travelers would put themselves in the care and protection of a "coach" to get to a desired location they could not arrive at on their own. Thus, a sports coach is someone who takes young student-athletes where they cannot take themselves.

Society tends to have a myopic view of a coach as someone hired to train a team to win games. Coaches are usually former athletes who are committed to teaching skills and strategies to help others experience success in a sport that they enjoyed and in which they experienced affirming accolades during their playing careers. Like it or not, society shines a very bright spotlight on athletic stadiums and arenas, where many eyes are watching and reading about the performance of athletes and their coaches. The Christian recognizes the opportunity to use his or her calling as a coach to utilize athletics as a platform to help athletes, regardless of their faith, develop positive virtues to forge strong character so they will become positive assets in society. In addition, the Christian coach can boldly carry out Christ's Great Commission by making verbal or nonverbal witness for Jesus Christ through his or her interactions with athletes and fans.

Coaching is a vocation that provides the opportunity for right-hand kingdom and left-hand kingdom work.[1] Since coaches tend to exert enormous influence over young people, they have a special responsibility and opportunity to share the Gospel as well as to teach and model good character. Coaches' influence in this regard is not limited to their athletes but also includes the student-athletes' families, school community, and the community at large. This privilege of being a beacon of light in the lives of many behooves them to maintain a Christ-centered perspective, which in turn compels them to speak and act in ways that honor the Lord and elevate their athletes.

Iconic coaches, like legendary basketball coach John Wooden from UCLA, embrace the opportunity to use athletics as the platform to teach many valuable life lessons such as teamwork, sacrifice, determination, humility, resilience, forgiveness, grit, and work ethic. These virtues are building blocks for success in life long after one's competitive athletic career is over. Athletes who were fortunate enough to play for Coach Wooden often reminisce that the life lessons learned on the basketball court positively impacted their character, future success, and happiness far more than their win-loss records or number of trophies won.

Former San Francisco Giant pitcher Dave Dravecky recognized the powerful connection that existed between his life as a talented athlete

1 See David W. Loy's essay "Vocation, Work, and Human Flourishing" in this volume for a discussion of the doctrine of the two kingdoms.

and as a committed Christian. In 1988, Dave was diagnosed with cancer in his pitching arm and faced radical surgery to remove muscle tissue to stop the spread of the tumor. Dave inspired the athletic world as he tirelessly rehabilitated his arm to allow him to pitch again less than a year later. After winning his first game back by retiring 21 of the first 23 batters he faced on the mound, he threw his last pitch of his career only one week later when his humerus bone snapped. Following the tragedy, Dave said that breaking his arm actually gave him a larger platform for witnessing to Christ. It is refreshing to see how coaches like John Wooden and athletes like Dave Dravecky can expand society's viewpoint of athletics to encompass much more than simply striving to win games.

What Should Christians Know as They Enter the Coaching Profession?

There are many joys of coaching derived from working with athletes who are eager to excel and compete in a sport. Coaching is about people first—it is a calling that allows leaders to forge lasting relationships with athletes, the athletes' siblings and parents, and the community at large through many hours of working together. It is exhilarating to teach fundamental skills, integrate strategic plays, and then see them translate into success in competitive situations. It is truly rewarding to watch athletes navigate between the highs and lows associated with winning and losing while developing a lasting passion for their sport.

However, there are numerous challenges and pressures that coaches face today. First, it is increasingly clear that our society values winning games above all else with little regard for the character and integrity of the athlete winning those games. There are more coaches today than ever before, at all levels, who are being fired. Community, school, and professional sports leaders have little patience for losing teams and quickly affix blame on coaches. The pressure to win is relentless and pervasive.

Because the highs and lows experienced in athletics are often extreme, and because most coaches are judged by their win-loss record, it is natural and more common for coaches to be pressured to fall for the temptation of focusing exclusively on competitive results. This unhealthy perspective shifts the coach's attention from serving the eclectic needs of student-athletes to winning. Coaches frequently embrace the value of teaching the fundamental athletic skills in order to build and develop athletic success. This same truth applies in life; the fundamental life skills are even more important and crucial as they build and develop the student-athlete for an entire life of success and not just those good old "glory years."

In addition, many parents selfishly look first and foremost at how the sport is benefiting their individual child. Parents are sadly not as interested in what is best for the success of the entire team as much as they scrutinize their child's playing time, media exposure, and win-loss records. Parents covet individual recognition for their child to heighten chances for potential college scholarships or professional offers. Many parents also seem to use their child's success levels to bolster their own egos.

Because of this pressure from parents, there are many athletes who learn a me-first attitude. Athletes are quick to transfer to a new club, high school, or university for perceived personal benefits and advantages. Ubiquitous transfer rules at all levels endorse this mentality, empowering athletes to select new teams easily whenever they want. It takes concerted focus and unwavering commitment by today's coaches to teach athletes the importance of team first.

The challenge for coaches is to concentrate first and foremost on creating championship human beings rather than on chasing championship trophies. Just as Jesus taught that, paradoxically, if you want to be great, you must serve (Matthew 20:26), individuals who see coaching as a calling from the Lord understand that winning on the scoreboard is a by-product of meeting and serving the needs of their athletes first.

Some of the larger needs that athletes have include faith development, character formation, academic achievement, physical development, learning to commit to something greater than themselves, developing life grit, and having fun. When coaches are fixated on winning, it becomes difficult to channel energy toward meeting these needs. As the Russian proverb says, "If you chase two rabbits, you won't catch either one." Communicating and front-loading student-athletes, parents, and the community with these foundational life truths and vision can help give the coach's athletic community focus and purpose. These also become touch points when tough conversations arise. The Bible clearly teaches that we reap what we sow (Galatians 6:7); therefore, Christian coaches are called to sow Christlike characteristics and weave biblical life lessons into the lives of their student-athletes.

What Challenges Might Christian Coaches Face?

There are numerous challenges associated with the vocation of coaching. Any time you compete, there are temptations to become angry and frustrated. You do not have to watch too many ESPN highlights before you observe coaches swearing at referees, berating players, growling at reporters, or even throwing chairs across basketball courts. Christian coaches recognize the deleterious effects such behaviors have on their witness for Christ and will strive to discipline themselves to exude poise, class, and good sportsmanship.

Another challenge that seems to permeate the coaching profession is the tendency to develop a workaholic lifestyle. Winning is addictive. Addictions will lead to a loss of balance in life and poor self-care. It is not uncommon to find coaches suffering from poor diet, lack of exercise, lack of sleep, lack of time with family, and lack of time spent in worship. The pressure to avoid a poor win-loss record is a real factor that must be acknowledged and deliberately accounted for. Coaches must recognize that self-care is not selfish and take time for themselves.

Because members of society judge coaches by how much they win, temptations abound for coaches to operate from a win-at-all-costs mindset. This mindset poses numerous ethical temptations to win by compromising one's integrity, such as the following:

- Recruiting violations
- Paying referees

- Not fairly distributing playing time so the entire team feels involved
- Playing injured athletes when they should be rehabilitating
- Integrating performance enhancing drugs into athletes' routines
- Not maintaining proper training/rest ratios
- Accepting money or other gifts from parents for increased playing time
- Teaching athletes unethical or illegal techniques and tactics to gain advantages over opponents
- Manipulating athletes to ingest substances to unethically enhance and expedite their physical development
- Teaching athletes to denigrate or intimidate opponents

This list of behaviors poses a sad commentary on the sinful world we live in. Unfortunately, this list of sinful behaviors is more common than many innocent bystanders realize—and represents very real temptations that Christian coaches must flee from. A person's integrity is destroyed one small cut at a time; therefore, it must be diligently guarded in every decision. Coaches do well to establish a confidential integrity-accountability colleague; Christian colleagues can help one another keep Christ as their North Star.

How Does Being a Christian Inform a Calling as Coach?

The Christian who is called into the coaching profession has a huge platform on which to witness for Jesus Christ. The public eye is focused on athletes and is eager to pay money to watch them compete. The nonverbal, verbal, and written communication skills of the Christian coach can be utilized to show a commitment to live as Christ's disciple.

It is refreshing to see the following advice by Paul in Colossians 3:12 embraced by today's Christian coaches to exhibit Christlike virtues: "Put on then, as God's chosen ones, holy and beloved, compassionate hearts, kindness, humility, meekness, and patience."

Coach John Wooden knew the importance of witnessing for Christ as he led the UCLA Bruin basketball team to numerous accolades and NCAA championships. On game days, when the spotlight was the brightest, he made sure to place a small silver metal cross in his suit pocket. Any time Coach Wooden started to feel he was getting angry and losing his focus, he would stick his hand in his pocket to grasp the cross as a reminder of his commitment to use his vocation to be an active part of Christ's Great Commission. Coach Wooden knew that the most important thing in his life and the integral part of his vocation was his relationship with Christ. Coaches today need to take advantage of the awesome opportunities available to them to serve in the right-hand kingdom and left-hand kingdom to make a statement that their lives are guided by a much bigger calling than to just win games. Coaches are called to boldly live as disciples of Jesus Christ. Christian coaches have an internal purpose and calling that leads them to pass on an eternal life plan to their student-athletes and the generations that follow.

Being a devoted Christian has a dramatic impact on every key area of coaching leadership, including perspective, purpose, and principles. The perspective from which Christ-centered coaches operate compels them to see and understand what athletics can do for others and to define success in a way that is achievable for all within the team or program. Their purpose is centered around serving not only the short-term welfare of athletes but, more important, their long-term welfare. What godly coaches teach and engrave on the hearts of athletes will leave a positive impact on countless people and reinforce Christ's call to make disciples throughout the world.

References

Veith, G. E., Jr. (2002). *God at work.* Crossway.

THE VOCATION OF LAW AND THE PURSUIT OF JUSTICE

Jodi Nafzger

Jodi Nafzger, JD, is a Lutheran lawyer and educator in Boise, ID. She is the Director of Experiential Learning at The College of Idaho. She is a former prosecutor, police adviser, and Professor of legal ethics and criminal practice at Concordia University, Portland's School of Law and the University of Idaho College of Law.

A Noble Career Path

The different roles of the lawyer are summarized into three categories: representatives for clients, officers of the court, and public citizens with a special responsibility to preserve justice.[1] In short, these are the job description of the lawyer. Each role carries a responsibility that is distinct from other professions. Lawyers act on behalf of clients and play a vital role in the administration of justice. Preserving justice is arguably the most difficult role of the lawyer. After all, what is justice? Justice is defined most plainly as fair treatment for each person or the quality of being fair or right. Justice, then, is concerned with both truth and fairness. But what does it mean to preserve justice? Lawyers have a responsibility to uphold the legal system and ensure that the system produces just outcomes. In doing so, the ethical lawyer seeks the truth. But the system is flawed, in part because humans are fallible and sinful.

In his article *The Practice of Law as a Vocation or Calling*, Timothy Floyd concludes that justice is not only the lawyer's responsibility; rather, the legal system as a whole produces justice, and every judge, juror, attorney, client, and witness contributes to justice.[2] However, sometimes justice is miscarried, whether by police, prosecutors, defense attorneys, judges, or jurors, such as when a person is wrongly convicted of a crime. Miscarriages may be willful, as in the case of police misconduct, or unintentional, such as a juror who relies on mistaken

1 Model Rules of Prof'l Conduct, pmbl. (Am. Bar Ass'n 1983).

2 Timothy W. Floyd, *The Practice of Law as a Vocation or Calling*, 66 Fordham L. Rev. 1405 (1998), https://ir.lawnet.fordham.edu/flr/vol66/iss4/30.

eyewitness testimony. The legal system has inherent corrective measures including the right to an appeal and the right to postconviction relief until the remedies are exhausted. Nevertheless, truth is not always found and justice is not always served. Furthermore, justice cannot be served when millions of Americans lack meaningful access to courts, especially in civil cases where the right to counsel is not guaranteed.

Luther said the purpose of all vocations is to love and serve our neighbors.[3] Many lawyers believe by definition they serve their neighbors. Some are legal aid lawyers, civil rights lawyers, or public servants. Prosecutors in particular are considered ministers of justice.[4] A prosecutor's goal is to seek and present the truth, afford the accused procedural fairness, hold the guilty accountable, and protect the rights of victims. Defense counsel arguably have the more difficult task of serving as both officers of the court and advocates for their clients.[5] Defense attorneys may face tension between their duty to preserve justice as officers of the court and their duty to diligently and zealously advocate for their client.

God put us, even lawyers, on this earth to do His work. "For we are His workmanship, created in Christ Jesus for good works, which God prepared beforehand, that we should walk in them" (Ephesians 2:10). Luther extols work done in faith toward God over good works such as fasts, pilgrimages, attendance at masses, alms, and gifts to the church.

> Thus a Christian . . . who lives in this confidence toward God knows all things, can do all things, ventures everything that needs to be done, and does everything gladly and willingly, not that he may gather merits and good works, but because it is a pleasure for him to please God in doing these things. He simply serves God with no thought of reward, content that his service pleases God.[6]

---

3 Gene Edward Veith, Working for our Neighbor: A Lutheran Primer on Vocation, Economics, and Ordinary Life xvi (2016).

4 Model Rules of Prof'l Conduct, Rule 3.8, Comment 1 (1983).

5 ABA Criminal Justice Standards: Defense Function, Standard 4-1.2(b), Fourth Edition (2017).

6 *Luther's Works* 44:27.

How do lawyers do God's will? Understanding law as a helping profession might lend some answers to this question. A helping profession is one traditionally associated with extensive learning, preparation, and practice. Lawyers serve their clients sometimes during the most vulnerable times in their lives. In that work, lawyers owe their clients the fiduciary duties of loyalty and confidentiality.[7] Lawyers, we might say, are blessed with certain gifts of healing, helping, and guidance. Lawyers are also called to serve persons of limited means or those who cannot otherwise afford to hire a lawyer. Increasingly, even middle-income Americans cannot afford a lawyer's hourly rate.[8] Lawyers are becoming inaccessible to the general population. The responsibility of lawyers to help others is illustrated by the oath we take to serve the underserved. When new lawyers are sworn into the profession, we raise our right hand and promise that we will "contribute time and resources to public service, and will never reject . . . the cause of the defenseless or oppressed."[9] While oaths vary by state, the following example illustrates the spirit behind the lawyer's oath.

> I DO SOLEMNLY SWEAR THAT: . . . I will support the Constitution of the United States and the Constitution of the State.
>
> I will abide by the rules of professional conduct adopted by the Supreme Court.
>
> I will respect courts and judicial officers in keeping with my role as an officer of the court.
>
> I will represent my clients with vigor and zeal, and will preserve inviolate their confidences and secrets.
>
> I will never seek to mislead a court or opposing party

7 Model Rules of Prof'l Conduct, Rules 1.3, 1.6 (Am. Bar Ass'n 1983).

8 Debra Cassens Weiss, *Middle-Income Dilemma: Can't Afford Lawyers, Can't Qualify for Legal Aid*, ABA Journal (July 22, 2010, 1:36 PM), https://www.abajournal.com/news/article/middle-class_dilemma_cant_afford_lawyers_cant_qualify_for_legal_aid.

9 Idaho Bar Comm'n Rules r. 220 (Bd. of Comm'rs of the Idaho State Bar 1986).

> by false statement of fact or law, and will scrupulously honor promises and commitments made.
>
> I will attempt to resolve matters expeditiously and without unnecessary expense.
>
> *I will contribute time and resources to public service, and will never reject, for any consideration personal to myself, the cause of the defenseless or oppressed.*
>
> I will conduct myself personally and professionally in conformity with the high standards of my profession.
>
> SO HELP ME GOD. (I hereby affirm.)[10]

The oath acknowledges the esteem of the legal profession and prepares the incoming practitioner to contribute time and money to help people who are in need. Luther taught that if a person holds high office, that means that he has more people to serve than one who holds a lower office.[11] He taught us to fill the office which God has given us, as long as we have the strength to do so.[12] Lawyers are held to a higher standard in part because of our access to a learned and noble profession. In most states, lawyers are expected to contribute fifty hours of pro bono legal services each year. Pro bono services include providing direct legal services to underserved or marginalized individuals, providing services on behalf of nonprofit organizations and government agencies, or contributing resources to legal aid services and volunteer lawyer programs.

In the two-kingdoms framework, lawyers are serving in the left-hand kingdom.[13] The lawyer's function in that kingdom may include making laws to protect our communities, protecting society from harm and danger, defending the Constitution, and in the end, battling sin. Some scholars argue that the legal system is corrupt and that incidences

10 Idaho Bar Comm'n Rules r. 220 (Bd. of Comm'rs of the Idaho State Bar 1986), emphasis added.

11 *Luther's Works* 51:347–54.

12 *Id.*

13 See Martin Luther, *Temporal Authority: To What Extent It Should Be Obeyed* (1523), *Luther's Works* 45:75–129; see also David W. Loy, *Vocation, Work, and Human Flourishing* in this volume.

of judicial bribery are a significant problem in the United States.[14] Can a Christian participate in such corruption? The adversarial system resolves disputes by presenting conflicting evidence to an impartial decision maker.[15] Does not an adversarial system fail before a biased judge? Romans teaches that we all fall short and are made right with God by placing our faith in Jesus Christ (Romans 3:23–25). And this is true for everyone who believes, no matter who we are. Since we all fall short, it should be expected that no legal order will be without sin. Yet the Bible does not call Christians to leave the world; instead, since we are made right by placing our faith in Jesus Christ, we can boldly engage with these systems in hopes of serving our neighbors. Thus, the Old Testament prophets do not call on judges to give up being judges but instead to uphold the cause of the weak against those who introduce corruption into the system. God does not call us to leave the system or overthrow it but instead to operate within it with (1) faith in Christ, (2) love for neighbor, and (3) a desire to seek justice and peace within our limited sphere of influence (that is, within the parameters of our specific vocation).

The distinct roles of the lawyer's office are also explained in the preamble of the *Model Rules of Professional Conduct*.

> [1] A lawyer, as a member of the legal profession, is a representative of clients, an officer of the legal system and a public citizen having special responsibility for the quality of justice.
>
> . . .
>
> [6] As a public citizen, a lawyer should seek improvement of the law, access to the legal system, the administration of justice and the quality of service rendered by the legal profession. As a member of a learned profession, a lawyer should cultivate knowledge of the law

14 Stratos Pahis, *Corruption in Our Courts: What It Looks Like and Where It Is Hidden*, 118 YALE L.J. 1900 (2009).

15 Monroe Freedman, *Our Constitutionalized Adversary System*, CHAPMAN L. REV. 57 (1998).

> beyond its use for clients, employ that knowledge in reform of the law and work to strengthen legal education. In addition, a lawyer should further the public's understanding of and confidence in the rule of law and the justice system because legal institutions in a constitutional democracy depend on popular participation and support to maintain their authority. A lawyer should be mindful of deficiencies in the administration of justice and of the fact that the poor, and sometimes persons who are not poor, cannot afford adequate legal assistance. Therefore, all lawyers should devote professional time and resources and use civic influence to ensure equal access to our system of justice for all those who because of economic or social barriers cannot afford or secure adequate legal counsel. A lawyer should aid the legal profession in pursuing these objectives and should help the bar regulate itself in the public interest.[16]

Lawyers do God's work when they ethically serve their clients and seek justice. In the criminal system, for example, whether the lawyer is representing the government or the defendant, the lawyer's work representing their client in resolving the dispute contributes to the fair functioning of the legal system as a whole. Lawyers battle sin in an adversarial system. Where the system suffers from corruption, the Lutheran lawyer can battle sin and seek justice, and the believers are washed clean by God's forgiveness.

The Ethics of Law

By taking the oath, lawyers promise to abide by certain ethical standards. The legal profession is regulated by the Rules of Professional Conduct that are promulgated by the American Bar Association ("ABA")

16 Model Rules of Prof'l Conduct, pmbl. (Am. Bar Ass'n 1983).

and adopted and enforced by the state supreme court. The original 32 Canons of Professional Ethics were adopted by the ABA in 1908, based on the Code of Ethics adopted by the Alabama State Bar Association in 1887.[17] Alabama's early code was borrowed from the lectures of the Honorable George Sharswood, Dean of the law school of the University of Pennsylvania and later Chief Justice of the Pennsylvania Supreme Court, and from David Hoffman's 1836 book *A Course of Legal Study: Addressed to Students and the Profession Generally*.[18] Since the code's original adoption the ABA has incorporated a limited number of amendments on a piecemeal basis and, in 1969, adopted the *Model Code of Professional Responsibility*. In 1983, the ABA adopted the *Model Rules of Professional Conduct*, which replaced the *Model Code of Professional Responsibility* as the governing standards of professional responsibility for lawyers.[19]

The rules of professional conduct provide guidance as to the lawyer-client relationship; the lawyer's responsibility as counsel and advocate; the business aspects of the practice of law; and, more generally, maintaining the integrity of the profession.[20] A violation of these rules can subject a lawyer to discipline by the state supreme court. If a lawyer violates an ethical rule, the state bar association, through its Bar Counsel's Office, can investigate, charge, and discipline the lawyer. Sanctions may include private or public reprimands and suspension or even revocation of the lawyer's license to practice. The rules of professional conduct aim to protect the clients and the community from a lawyer's lack of competence, diligence, and good judgment.

The ethical rules are not an arbitrary set of limitations on the lawyer's practice. The rules are meant to protect society and clients from unethical lawyers. The rules reflect the conditions under which the

17 American Bar Association, *Final Report of the Committee on Code of Prof'l Ethics* 577, 569, https://www.americanbar.org/content/dam/aba/administrative/professional_responsibility/1908_code.pdf (last visited Oct. 21, 2023).

18 David Hoffman, A Course of Legal Study: Addressed to Students and the Profession Generally (2d ed. 1836).

19 Model Rules of Prof'l Responsibility, Preface (1999), http://www.americanbar.org/groups/professional_responsibility/publications/model_rules_of_professional_conduct/model_rules_of_professional_conduct_preface.html, last visited Oct. 21, 2023.

20 *Id.*

legal profession will actually be good for society. Luther teaches that the Christian is disposed to see a proper ethical course behind commonplace actions.[21] "It is one's neighbor, not one's sanctification, which stands at the heart of the ethics of vocation."[22] In particular, when a Lutheran lawyer ponders how to act in a certain set of circumstances, he can also rely on "sanctified common sense," which has been described as a balanced approach—"with sensitivity to the 'witness value' of a given action or activity in a specific context."[23]

God's Guidance for Lawyers

Lawyers benefit from the guidance of the supreme court, the oath, and the rules of professional conduct. The Bible also speaks to the individual's role to serve our neighbors. The story of the Good Samaritan is emblematic of this role. This parable from the book of Luke is preceded by a conversation between Jesus and a lawyer, or at least an expert in the law. In the parable, the lawyer asks Jesus what he must do to inherit eternal life. Jesus responds by asking the lawyer to consider what is written in the law. The lawyer answers, "You shall love the Lord your God with all your heart and with all your soul and with all your strength and with all your mind, and your neighbor as yourself" (Luke 10:27). When the lawyer inquires further about how to love his neighbor, Jesus responds with the parable of the Good Samaritan. The lawyer now sees clearly that the one who had mercy on the man who fell into the hands of robbers is loving his neighbor as himself. Jesus asks the lawyer to "go, and do likewise" (Luke 10:37).

The parable of the Good Samaritan is understood by some theologians Christologically, with the Samaritan representing Jesus.[24] Others believe the parable more generally represents the ethics of Jesus.[25] Overall, the parable teaches about service, empathy, and mercy as interpreted by an expert in the law.

21 Gustaf Wingren, Luther on Vocation 181 (1957).

22 *Id.* at 182.

23 The Lutheran Church—Missouri Synod, FAQs about LCMS Views, https://www.lcms.org/about/beliefs/faqs/lcms-views (last visited July 2021).

24 See Arthur A. Just Jr., Luke 9:51-24:53, Concordia Commentary Series, 454–55 (1997).

25 See Darrel L. Bock, Luke 9:51-24:53, Baker Exegetical Commentary on the New Testament, 1035 (1996).

While the rules of professional conduct for lawyers speak to the need to develop one's own moral compass to resolve ethical questions, Luther teaches Christians to look to the Scriptures for guidance on moral decision-making. The Bible's guidance makes it clear that our moral decision-making should always account for the well-being of our neighbor—whoever that is in a given vocation—and in fact to prioritize our neighbor's well-being over our own.

God's Plan for Lawyers

The central roles of the lawyer—representative of clients, officer of the court, and public citizen with special responsibilities—can be in tension with the Scriptures. A lawyer may be called upon to handle a divorce, defend an individual accused of murder or child abuse, or fight discrimination based on a protected class, a constitutional protection with which he or she may disagree.

Consider this example. Thom is accused of murdering his spouse. Police found the murder weapon in Thom's car. Latent fingerprint tests from the scene and the weapon came back from the laboratory as Thom's match. Unfortunately for the prosecution, the police botched the investigation. When they interviewed Thom, they did not provide him with Miranda warnings.[26] Although Thom confessed to the murder, the confession may not be admissible. Also, police detectives searched Thom's car without first obtaining a warrant signed by a judge, so the prosecutor may not be able to introduce that evidence at trial. Aliza has been appointed as Thom's public defender. Aliza is a Christian. She knows Thom committed the crime. He confessed to the crime and his fingerprints were all over the scene. Her responsibility as a public defender requires her to bring a legal challenge to the confession and the illegal search. If she wins those arguments in front of a judge, she will represent Thom at trial. The Bible teaches, "You shall not murder" (Exodus 20:13) and "you shall accept no ransom for the

26 The requirement to give Miranda warnings came from the United States Supreme Court decision *Miranda v. Arizona*, 384 US 436 (1966). "Miranda warnings" refer to the constitutional requirement that once an individual is detained by the police, a police officer is required to give the individual certain warnings about their right to remain silent and their right to an attorney.

life of a murderer, who is guilty of death" (Numbers 35:31). How does Aliza reconcile her faith with her duty to represent Thom?

An essential function of the adversarial system is to protect individual human rights. The right to counsel is "the most precious" of rights because it affects one's ability to assert any other right.[27] The defense attorney's job in advocating for his or her client is not necessarily to argue that the client is innocent but rather to protect the client's constitutional rights, to mitigate harm to the client's life and liberty, and to seek the sanction that will best rehabilitate the client. Some scholars suggest that criminal defense attorneys help the prosecution find the objective truth in the case.[28] In this role, defense attorneys seek out information in possession of the prosecution and police and identify exculpatory evidence or impeachment evidence that may absolve their client or mitigate punishment.[29]

Put simply, guilty people have rights too. The United States Constitution protects the rights of the accused, affords the accused the right to counsel, and requires due process of law before loss of life, liberty, or property. Rights like trial by jury and the assistance of counsel are most important when the accused stands alone against the government. Each party takes up a role in the adversarial system and the search for truth and justice. Similarly, in the civil legal system, the adversarial system is effective in addressing the grievances of minorities, women, consumers, tenants, and environmental concerns.[30]

In some ways, Aliza's defense of Thom reflects the Old Testament practice of permitting an individual guilty of involuntary manslaughter to flee to a "city of refuge" to avoid death (Exodus 21:12–13; Numbers 35:9–34; Deuteronomy 19:1–13). The right to flee protected the guilty party from excessive punishment by the family of the victim. The so-called lex talionis of Leviticus 24:19–20 ("If anyone injures his

27 Walter V. Schaefer, *Federalism and State Criminal Procedure*, 70 HARV. L. REV. 1, 8 (1957), quoted with approval in *United States v. Cronic*, 466 US 648, 654 (1984).

28 JOHN KAPLAN, CRIMINAL JUSTICE 264–65 (1973); Jesse Berman, *The Cuban Popular Trials*, 69 COLUM. L. REV. 1317, 1341 (1969).

29 STANDARDS FOR CRIMINAL JUSTICE 4-4.1 (ABA 1979).

30 *Supra* 16 at 64.

neighbor, as he has done it shall be done to him, . . . eye for eye") also protected guilty individuals from excessive punishment.[31] Because Thom stands against the government as an accused, he is in danger of having his rights violated. Aliza stands up for him to ensure his rights are preserved and that where the police violated those rights, Thom is defended. In this way, she serves God by serving Thom.

Conclusion

Lawyers who practice ethically contribute to a just society. Lawyers are called to use their education to serve their neighbors, and they have a special responsibility to serve the underserved. In all of their work, lawyers can do God's work in the kingdom of the world. Without lawyers, the adversarial system breaks down and individual human rights are not preserved.

31 On the importance of justice in the Old Testament, see Paul Elliott's essay "The Working God in the Old Testament" in this volume.

A CHRISTIAN APPROACH TO WORKING IN BUSINESS

Christopher "Kit" Nagel

Kit Nagel is Professor of Business and Economics at Concordia University Irvine. His courses include International Marketing, International Finance, Global Enterprise, and Marketing Research. His corporate experience includes the positions of Marketing Manager—Asia for International Paper Company and VP—Commercial Development for Servrite International. He has worked and traveled throughout the world and negotiated with governments at the ministerial level. His writings on trade are published by Pearson Education, and his primer, Global Market Entry, *is assigned by global firms to those newly tasked with international responsibilities.*

This chapter is written from the perspective of a business professor and former marketing manager for a Fortune 100 and—perhaps not surprisingly—a proponent of free markets. The intent is to look at how one's actions in business can be informed by the Lutheran tradition and the doctrine of vocation. We will weave together several threads that reflect Martin Luther's view on how we should deal with others. We'll look at the challenge of facing ethical issues (that will surely arise in your career); we'll comment on a productive approach to negotiating agreements; and we'll look at how one should relate to those who will report to you, their supervisor or manager. Fundamentally, the theme of this chapter is on how one chooses to deal with clients, suppliers, and fellow workers.

On the Lutheran Tradition

First, we should provide a note here on the Lutheran tradition. Lutherans are known to use the term "vocation," which means "to be called" and comes from the Latin *vocatio*. Our calling is first to serve God, and beyond that, God works through us in the world to provide for the needs of others, both believers and nonbelievers.

Lutheranism, at its core, is a confession of faith, a theological movement. To claim the name Lutheran is to affirm a theological grounding that guides and shapes doctrine, faith, life, practice, mission, and direction.[1] As Christians and as managers, we all need to navigate and operate in the broader world. And we should think about what it is to behave in a right and proper way.

Swedish theologian Bo Giertz notes that all people have "common sense, including a sense of right and wrong." And he is talking about all people, across cultures. We are free to decide how we should act, even though it is also in our nature to stray from what we know we ought to do. And yet, we all have "the power to choose the good and do it."[2] So let's here talk about one's direction in life and, yes, about choosing the good. Your behavior for the greater good in the professions does matter. As the apostle John wrote, "Let us not love in word or talk but in deed and in truth" (1 John 3:18).

Martin Luther's theologically based approach to life and business is *Nächstenliebe* (pronounced NECKS-ten-lee-bah), which loosely translates as the necessary love and care for those together with us in society, our fellow citizens. The reader should reflect on this *Nächstenliebe* throughout this short chapter—and throughout life. Luther is best remembered as a doctor of theology, but he wrote with keen insight about the commercial world around him. He noted the beneficial and self-regulating role of a free market, where goods should be valued at the price derived from the give and take in the marketplace. Luther considered any profit made in this way toward earning a modest living as honest and proper. Even back in the sixteenth century, Luther recognized that merchants could fairly price-in risk to their sales price—a modern concept. He also, perhaps surprisingly, understood finance and compound interest, something two-thirds of Americans even today do not understand.[3]

1 See Stephen P. Mueller, "Distinctives of Lutheran Theology for Higher Education," in *The Idea and Practice of a Christian University*, ed. Scott A. Ashmon (St. Louis: Concordia Publishing House, 2015), 79.

2 Bo Giertz, *The Freedom We Have in Christ* (London: Concordia, 1962), 1. This is from the lecture Giertz delivered at the inauguration of Westfield House as a Lutheran House of Studies in Cambridge, England.

3 See Alexander Conrad, "Finance Basics Elude Citizens," *The Harvard Crimson*, February 28, 2008.

In Luther's time there was a broad and often justified perception of merchant fraud, and Luther spoke out strongly when he saw common people abused. When Luther saw merchants taking advantage of buyers, he called them *Geytzige blassen* ("greedy-bloated fellows"),[4] and he was especially harsh on the large financial houses that grew fat manipulating markets with impunity. Luther would call those managers *Stuhlräuber* ("armchair bandits").[5]

In our time, we see fraud around us: major banks gaming LIBOR, or Goldman Sachs peddling dodgy mortgage-backed securities (and paying a five-billion-dollar settlement). Poster child for the lack of Luther's *Nächstenliebe* is Lehman Brothers, which manipulated markets for short-term gain. The firm was led by Richard Fuld, who, while flying his company into failure and helping crater the US economy, "got his" in taking out earnings of $71.9 million. In your career, you will see such managers with a destructive and pathetic lack of Luther's *Nächstenliebe*.

It may sound old school, but a business manager's role is to act for the good of society—what George Vojta, the former chair of the Board of Governors of the Federal Reserve System, called "service to clients and service to society."[6] As managers, we should teach and admonish those who report to us to be honorable citizens and always to consider the impact on those with whom they will deal, and again, to follow Luther's *Nächstenliebe*, the love and care for those together with us in society, our fellow citizens, our neighbors.

On Ethics and Right Behavior

Now let's take a look at the broader world. The author has traveled and worked in over fifty countries and has observed a remarkably universal code of ethics—a sense of right and wrong—across cultures and across borders. This innate sense of what is right and wrong is there, whether people follow that in their daily lives or not. This is a truth that is grounded in Scripture and affirmed by Luther in the

4 *Luther's Works* 45:298.

5 Kolb-Wengert, Large Catechism I 228.

6 The author is grateful for the generous assistance of George Vojta, Vice Chair (ret.), Bankers Trust.

Large Catechism, saying that when God created people, He wrote the law in their hearts.[7] Here Luther is referencing natural law that applies to all, not just Christians. And this truth flows from both the Old and New Testaments, as Paul wrote: "the work of the law is written on their hearts" (Romans 2:15).

At a fundamental level, all peoples recognize that one should be truthful and that graft and corruption are wrong. The real question is actually one of degree—what is the level of tolerance by a person or society for wrongdoing? So when an American manager overseas seeks to act with integrity, I dismiss the notion that he or she is an agent of Western cultural imperialism trying to impose his or her own version of ethics. Such natural law is universal.

In your career you will see corruption. As managers, we are led to the question, "We're here to do a job, but how should we operate?" In getting things done overseas, sometimes baksheesh or, to use a more benign word, a gratuity is asked for. In some countries this is called "grease," in Mexico, a "mordida," or in Nigeria, the charming term "dash."

In many countries, this is an everyday part of living. In India, graft has almost standard rates. If you want a landline to your house, you can have it next week (that is, if you pay the foreman a set gift level of five thousand rupees) or you can wait half a year. Which would you prefer? Or after you pay your taxes, the municipal clerk is supposed to endorse a voucher showing that you have paid. However, for that action you need to give him a gratuity on top of the taxes. If you do not pay, the voucher will be lost somewhere in the bureaucracy, and as you will be unable to prove you have paid your taxes, you will be in violation of the law. In their hearts, both the foreman and the bureaucrat know this is wrong.

So how should one proceed? For long-term success in business, you should have a backbone and not go with the flow or just take the easy way. Be the salt of the earth, be someone known to do the right thing, and you will be trusted, which, in truth, will be the vital currency in your career.

7 Large Catechism II 67.

An important takeaway from conversations with senior managers is that in dealings with leaders in both industry and government—when the issue of effective leadership comes up—few qualities are mentioned with greater force or frequency than integrity. It is the social cement of the leader-follower dynamic. Making a financial or personal investment in someone is a leap of faith and trust. It is where leadership meets reality. Most investors, company CEOs, and government officials place a premium on honesty and trustworthiness in making decisions on investments or partnerships. This is also a truth.

The more experienced the manager, the more he or she knows well enough to walk away from potentially lucrative deals when a sense of trust has not been developed. If there is no trust or integrity, success is at best temporary and limited. Lasting success is built on repeated interaction—and in this digital world, major business is still done old school, with those you trust and have had success with before. Cheat me once, shame on me; cheat me twice, and the entire industry will know about you. That is another truth. It is also a truth that once your credibility is questioned, rebuilding it is almost impossible.

Ethics and integrity go beyond adherence to laws governing your industry or business. Ethics go beyond borders and cultures and are aligned with the higher universal truth noted above. Ethics should not be a risk-benefit calculation—adjusting the degree of compliance with the benefits or risks involved. Now, you may ask, that is a nice and laudable philosophy, but is it real world? In theological terminology, we live in a fallen world and an often corrupt world. And this leads to the question, can a business act ethically and prosper? Or from a more liberal perspective, are businesses in market economies even capable of acting ethically? The answer to these questions is yes—and it is a real-world yes.

Here is an example: a friend is a senior executive at a major pharmaceutical company in Europe, and his firm exported an important cholesterol-lowering therapy into a Western-European country. However, the shipments got held up in customs by officials looking to shake down the company. My friend took the issue to the highest levels in the government. The ministers listened and smiled and told him they were sure he could work it out, but they did not act. The manager then put a hold on further drug shipments to doctors and hospitals. This understandably created a groundswell of concern in the medical community that the press picked up on, which then shamed the government ministries into clearing the shipments.[8] Obviously, such ethical calls are not the road of least resistance or of getting along. They are difficult, but they lead to change. Today that country's officials know better than to try again to shake down his company. The lesson is that when one's position is clear, that corruption and collusion are not common practice, then it will not be attempted. Fundamentally, the executive said, "As for me and my company, we will act ethically." And yes, this was an intentional and direct echo of Scripture: "As for me and my house, we will serve the Lord" (Joshua 24:15).

On Business Agreements

Seasoned managers know that, at the end of the day, negotiations and agreements should benefit both parties. Another friend, a brilliant engineer who was the Director of International Operations at Pratt and Whitney (jet engines), would often talk about outcomes in negotiations and business. He said that it is fundamentally important that a well-structured deal should be beneficial for all sides, and that the measure of success should not be a zero-sum game. In the real business world, it should not be about your side winning or out-negotiating your "opponent." Instead, managers in the Fortune 500 look for long-term, mutually beneficial relationships. This is not only *Nächstenliebe* but leads to lasting success.

. . . and on Lawyers

We'll pivot here and look at the American cultural approach to business negotiations—aided and abetted by lawyers—and yes, in the context of Luther's *Nächstenliebe*. We'll also add a phrase one learns to live by growing up Lutheran: to "put the best construction on everything." This

8 The author is grateful for the generous assistance of Dieter Weinand, a C-level executive in pharma.

comes from Luther's Small Catechism on the Eighth Commandment: "You shall not give false testimony against your neighbor." Luther then adds the follow-up question, "What does this mean?" to which he answers, "We should fear and love God that we may not deceitfully belie, betray, slander, nor defame our neighbor, but defend him, speak well of him, and put the best construction on everything."[9]

This is a good life lesson: we should not meet strangers with fear or suspicion but instead treat them as we would wish to be treated (obviously, a biblical approach). It is not that legalities don't have their place, but in the author's decades of management and sales experience, entering into a client relationship while putting the best construction on clients' motives leads to success more often than when entering with suspicion and a cadre of lawyers. Straight dealing and trust are reciprocated.

Too many American businesses have a fixation on contracts and legalities, something that is truly out of step with the rest of the world, which is the other 96 percent of the world's population. This is a great distraction and cause of inefficiency. In most cultures, unlike the United States, when an issue arises, the default position is *not* to bring in the lawyers. Of course, difficulties will arise, but they are most efficiently worked out between reasonable managers who value the relationship.

Focusing on legalities instead of putting the best construction on everything is a typically American perspective, and it is what sociologists call a low-context perspective. As a result, America is blessed with more lawyers per capita than any other country, and we are the most litigious nation on earth.

So how many lawyers is too many?

A Harvard Law study notes that the United States has 391 lawyers per 100,000 people; the Brits have 251, the French have 72, the Japanese have 23.[10] Obviously, these are all advanced societies where citizens

9 Small Catechism, 1943 edition. More recent translations say to "explain everything in the kindest way."

10 J. Mark Ramseyer and Eric B. Rasmusen, *Comparative Litigation Rates* (Harvard John M. Olin Discussion Paper Series, No. 681, Nov. 2010), http://nrs.harvard.edu/urn-3:HUL.InstRepos:30064400.

have rights and legal recourse. And yes, there are honorable Lutheran lawyers. But it does raise the question whether society benefits from so many capable minds being siphoned away from becoming engineers, scientists, or supply-chain managers and instead using their intellectual gifts for confrontation. The same might be said for the PhD-level quants being recruited by the financial houses to create esoteric financial products like leveraged ETFs, which invest not in productive capacity—like building more-efficient jet engines—but in volatility itself.

The writer has observed both businesses and investors who seem to be perennially in litigation, an incredible waste of time. It perhaps makes more sense to minimize litigation in the first place. And this also begs another question: why are some business people so adversarial?

That's hard to answer. Perhaps it is popular culture? Perhaps vested bar association interests? Perhaps so many lawyers beget even more lawyers? Even in academia college textbooks on business strategy discuss negotiations from a negative rather than constructive perspective. One need not be naïve, and of course there are sharp operators (Luther's *Stuhlräuber*), but business texts sadly inject unnecessary fear by describing your negotiating counterparts as having the traits of "opportunism" and "guile," which in the author's view is unnecessarily negative.[11] Again, a well-structured deal is one where both parties are satisfied and benefit. Success in the B2B is not about some simplistic idea of out-negotiating your opponent but about only (obviously) entering into deals where rapport and mutual trust have been established—yes, *Nächstenliebe*. It is actually not that complicated.

Some companies get the balance right. The in-house counsel at the writer's former company (a Fortune 100) would make the point that lawyers, who are not trained to understand markets or business strategy, should not lead or "drive the bus" in negotiations, telling the commercial managers, "You go make the commercial deal; we'll make it legal."

The apostle Paul (himself a trained lawyer) has a wise word for managers: he advises us "to avoid quarreling, to be gentle, . . . to show

11 Frank T. Rothaermel, *Strategic Management*, 6th ed. (New York: McGraw Hill, 2023), 305.

perfect courtesy toward all people . . . [and to] avoid foolish controversies, genealogies, dissensions, and quarrels about the law, for they are unprofitable and worthless" (Titus 3:2, 9).

On Your Employees

This last section will touch on the important question of how to deal with one's subordinates, those who will rely on you for their livelihood, to pay their mortgages, and to support their families. Here again one's actions can be informed by Luther's *Nächstenliebe* and the care one should have for those with us in society. Luther wrote that mistreatment of others is a form of theft, that is, "taking advantage of our neighbors in any sort of dealings that result in loss to them[,] . . . taking advantage of someone in the market . . . and . . . wherever business is transacted and money is exchanged for goods or services."[12] There is also biblical clarity on relations with one's employees:

> You shall not oppress a hired worker who is poor and needy. (Deuteronomy 24:14)
>
> Do not rob the poor, because he is poor. (Proverbs 22:22)

This is not about legalities but about love, ethics, and how to properly treat people. Business models do not happen in a vacuum; they are built out by management. For example, two successful retail companies, Costco and Walmart, each take a different approach to their workers. The reader may reflect upon which of these two retail giants has the greater sense of *Nächstenliebe*. In your own managerial judgment, toward which of the following models would you lean?

Costco is the sixth largest retailer in the world and the third largest in the United States, behind Walmart and Amazon. Costco management has built a company with a reputation as a good place to work, with industry-leading pay and benefits, a generous 401(k) plan, and a career track. Walmart management has not earned such a reputation—in fact its reputation is one of squeezing both its suppliers and employees at every turn. In contrast, Costco has been ranked among the best large

12 Kolb-Wengert, Large Catechism I 224.

employers and first in the large retail and wholesale category; Walmart consistently ranks in the bottom tier.

Any management course worth its salt will stress long-term success. And to appeal to workers, employers need to offer a living wage and a company culture that centers around valuing and respecting employees, things that Costco management seems to understand.

Both firms are profit-making and operate in the free market—and how they choose to operate is their legal prerogative. As rankings can be subjective, we should look for basic hard data on how Walmart treats its employees. One metric is to look at its reliance on the federal SNAP (Supplemental Nutrition Assistance Program, or food stamps) to support its business model.

In 2020 the nonpartisan US Government Accountability Office did an analysis on the use of SNAP by nine million individuals, 70 percent of whom work full time. Beyond the national data, the study also looked at SNAP usage in states across the country and listed the top twenty-five companies that employ the largest amount of people using SNAP in each of those states. Overwhelmingly across the country, Walmart ranked first or second in SNAP usage by its employees. (Costco never makes it onto those lists.) Surprisingly, even in Walmart's home state of Arkansas, over 3 percent of Arkansas workers who rely on federal food stamps are employed by Walmart.[13]

In contrast to Luther's and the Bible's admonitions (above) about how one should treat workers, the reader may perhaps judge that the Walmart model takes advantage of the struggling poor, those desperate enough to take a job to support their families where—by definition—Walmart does not provide a living wage. Free market advocates should be troubled when a for-profit's business model relies on government monies from taxpayers to subsidize its payroll, and the savings then flow to increase its bottom line and stockholder dividends. Walmart has the legal prerogative to do what they do, and this writer does not

13 US Government Accountability Office, *Federal Social Safety Net Programs: Millions of Full-Time Workers Rely on Federal Health Care and Food Assistance Programs*, GAO-21-45 (Washington, DC: October 2020).

begrudge paying taxes to support food stamps for the needy. And yet . . .

A closing comment, taking Luther's admonition in business life to put the "best construction on everything": your workers are not your enemy; your suppliers are not your enemy; your customers are not your enemy. We are actually all in this together.

This intent of this chapter was to provide a practitioner's perspective on what is both appropriate and productive behavior in business as informed by the Lutheran Christian tradition, and specifically on ethics, negotiating agreements, and dealing with one's clients, suppliers, and fellow workers. We will end here where we began, noting that we all have "the power to choose the good and do it."

THE VOCATION OF PHARMACIST

Nancy A. Stoehr

Dr. Nancy A. Stoehr, PharmD, MEd, BCSCP, FACA, is Associate Professor of Pharmaceutical Sciences and Director of Admissions for the School of Pharmacy at Concordia University Wisconsin. She has served Christian Pharmacists Fellowship International in various capacities since her days as a pharmacy student. Stoehr carries out her vocation through teaching and research focused in the areas of stability and quality of compounded dosage forms, formulation development, and spirituality in healthcare.

The pharmacist is a trained medical professional who uses extensive knowledge of medications and medication therapies to enhance the health and wellness of all patients. A primary responsibility of the pharmacist is to utilize her knowledge to educate patients and other healthcare practitioners regarding medication administration, side effects, or drug interactions. A pharmacist earns a Doctorate in Pharmacy at an accredited graduate institution before taking several licensure examinations. This licensure and terminal degree designate the pharmacist as the healthcare specialist responsible for the safe and accurate dispensing of medication, assurance of medication effectiveness, appropriate use of medications, and correct dosages of medication therapies. However, the pharmacist is more than the medications he works with; he is also a healthcare advocate. The pharmacist is the most easily accessible healthcare practitioner in the United States, as every corner drug store employs at least one pharmacist. Some of the skills, traits, and talents that a pharmacist uses to serve patients are learned behaviors, while others are God-given gifts. Learned skills are introduced and reinforced throughout the pharmacy school curriculum. God-given gifts are discovered, shaped, mentored, and refined throughout the pharmacist's lifetime.

Concordia University Wisconsin School of Pharmacy is committed to the development of pharmacists who are servant-leaders, dedicated to providing value-based, patient-centered care that improves the health of communities in rural and urban areas through excellence in teaching, research, service, and practice. Learning at a Christian institution of higher education allows students to explore the Christian faith and its connection to health and wellness openly and honestly in the classroom.

Every pharmacy graduate is encouraged to take a professional oath. This "Oath of a Pharmacist" reminds the graduate that being a pharmacist is not only an occupation—it is a life-changing commitment. The oath reads,

> I promise to devote myself to a lifetime of service to others through the profession of pharmacy. In fulfilling this vow: I will consider the welfare of humanity and relief of suffering my primary concerns. I will apply my knowledge, experience, and skills to the best of my ability to assure optimal outcomes for my patients. I will respect and protect all personal and health information entrusted to me. I will accept the lifelong obligation to improve my professional knowledge and competence. I will hold myself and my colleagues to the highest principles of our profession's moral, ethical and legal conduct. I will embrace and advocate changes that improve patient care. I will utilize my knowledge, skills, experiences, and values to prepare for the next generation of pharmacists.[1]

A pharmacist voluntarily makes the choice to live and abide by this oath. Note that the oath specifically states that the duty of pharmacist is to "serve." Choosing to serve and to respond to societal needs freely and with passion shows an understanding of the field of pharmacy as not only an occupation but a vocation. The great theologian Martin

1 AACP Board of Directors and the APhA Board of Trustees, "Oath of a Pharmacist," https://www.pharmacist.com/About/Oath-of-a-Pharmacist (accessed October 21, 2023).

Luther explains that God cares for people directly through the vocational callings of the individual. A Christian pharmacist who responds to God's calling to live out her vocation is joyous in her work, humbled to have the opportunity to serve, and consistently looking for ways by which to improve her craft. It may be difficult for some to see God in everyday, mundane activities. Yet, even during these activities God Himself is working in our lives. The God we cannot see is Himself at work through the people who are serving Him by serving the people around them. God is hidden behind but present within the good works done by ordinary people. In other words, God hides behind the "mask" of a person in a vocation and does His work through that person. The work of individuals within the professions allows God to touch each of His creatures on a personal level through such humble means as another human being.[2]

God uses the mask of the pharmacist to serve His creation through love by healing the body. God answers prayers for healing through the vocation of the pharmacist, who interacts with each patient, and through the medication touched by that pharmacist's hand. God has the power to heal directly through miracles, but more often He uses people to demonstrate His healing power. It is through this healing power, given by God, that pharmacists practice their vocation. When God uses flawed humans, prone to sin as they are, to provide and care for other human beings, He is clearly demonstrating His power and glory.

Often a pharmacist is called to wear multiple masks to accomplish the good that God has in mind for those who are being served. The vocations of Christian and pharmacist complement each other very well; Christian pharmacists have been blessed through the fruit of the Holy

2 See Matthew 25:34–40: "Then the King will say to those on His right, 'Come, you who are blessed by My Father, inherit the kingdom prepared for you from the foundation of the world. For I was hungry and you gave Me food, I was thirsty and you gave Me drink, I was a stranger and you welcomed Me, I was naked and you clothed Me, I was sick and you visited Me, I was in prison and you came to Me.' Then the righteous will answer Him, saying, 'Lord, when did we see You hungry and feed You, or thirsty and give You drink? And when did we see You a stranger and welcome You, or naked and clothe You? And when did we see You sick or in prison and visit You?' And the King will answer them, 'Truly, I say to you, as you did it to one of the least of these My brothers, you did it to Me.'"

Spirit to show Christian empathy toward others.[3] Speaking personally, my experiences in the vocations of mother, wife, daughter, and friend enhance and supplement my professional vocation. Being a wearer of many masks brings a distinct perspective to each situation. I have recognized that my approach to medication therapy has changed now that I have my own family. I am better able to empathize with parents of sick children. I understand the challenges faced when caregivers are attempting to dose a child with an unpalatable medication. I can recognize the pain felt by a daughter whose mother is sick with cancer or a wife whose husband is facing surgery.

There are other times when my vocations as pharmacist and mother collide. When my daughter was four years old, she had a tonsillectomy. Postsurgery, my daughter woke from the anesthesia in a delirium and was terrified. My vocation at that moment could only be 100 percent mom. However, the nurse who was caring for my daughter was unfamiliar with pediatric dosing of medications. The nurse also knew that I was a pharmacist, and when I instructed that she give a dose of medication, she looked to me for dosing information. The nurse was very appropriate in her vocational roles. She was serving her patient the best she could using the resources she had at hand. Unfortunately, that resource was me, the mother of the patient. The struggle in that moment between my vocation as mom and my vocation as pharmacist professional is still very present in my mind. I knew the answer to the dosing question clinically, but I did not know the answer maternally, and those two perspectives were in conflict. My pharmacist brain said, "Start low. Go slow." My mom brain said, "This child is in agony. Give her anything that calms her." With crisis comes the need for immediate action. We only have the liberty and privilege of reflection after the crisis has passed. Fortunately, all ended up well for my daughter. However, I learned that when my primary vocational role must be as a mother, I do not want to accept the responsibility of my vocational

3 The apostle Paul writes in 2 Corinthians 1:3–5, "Blessed be the God and Father of our Lord Jesus Christ, the Father of mercies and God of all comfort, who comforts us in all our affliction, so that we may be able to comfort those who are in any affliction, with the comfort with which we ourselves are comforted by God. For as we share abundantly in Christ's sufferings, so through Christ we share abundantly in comfort too."

role as pharmacy professional. Nor should I have to accept that responsibility. When my mind is mother first, it is important to remember that there are other health professionals living out their vocations using their gifts and talents to serve. Upon reflection, the competition between vocations seems clear. In that instance, my primary vocation was to my daughter, not the nurse who was taking care of my daughter. I should have kindly instructed the nurse to get help from another health professional rather than attempting to serve as that health professional myself. Recognizing roles and responsibilities is critical experiential wisdom to bring into our vocations.

The pharmacist working behind the counter in the community has the skill and knowledge to dispense medication to make the patient well. The pharmacist working with the federal government has the ability to influence lawmakers to create rules and regulations that improve public health. The pharmacist working with the dying child has talents and gifts to provide comfort for both the patient and the patient's family in their greatest time of need. God uses the pharmacist's talents and skill to care for other people. However, just because a pharmacist is using the skills he has to complete the activities required of him in his job does not necessarily mean he is living out his vocation as a pharmacist. There are plenty of pharmacists who perform the requirements of their job well but do not perform these tasks out of love or a desire to serve others. For these individuals, being employed as a pharmacist is simply a way to earn a living. This is not vocational observance. These individuals are not living out a vocation through pharmacy; they are simply living.[4]

One does not have be a Christian to live out a vocation.[5] Non-Christians can live out vocations in pharmacy using their talents and gifts by the grace of God just as Christian pharmacists can. The Christian pharmacist differs in that she uses those talents and gifts with the understanding that she loves and serves others because God first loved and served her through Christ. God's gifts to the Christian pharmacist can shine through in forgiveness for the demeaning physician or

4 Which is not to say that God does not work through such individuals. He does.

5 On this question, see David W. Loy's essay "Vocation, Work, and Human Flourishing" in this volume.

grace to the hostile patient. The Christian pharmacist can persevere in joy when the body and mind are tired because his soul is at rest. The Christian pharmacist can see beyond the pain and suffering of death that immediately await some patients. She can help the patient look beyond this life to the next life with God in eternity.

Most individuals seeking healthcare feel some sort of distress, whether emotional, physical, or spiritual. In healthcare, the ability to immediately emotionally sense how another is feeling allows true communication to begin. When the mother and her teenage daughter come to the pharmacy with a prescription for an abortifacient, whom do you counsel? The mother, who is worried about the health, future, and safety of her daughter? The daughter, who has made a difficult and terrifying decision? The unborn child, who has no voice of his or her own? In that moment, whose needs are greatest? Is it an emotional, physical, or spiritual need? Being able to recognize the type of need, as well as understand the situation from the patient's perspective, allows the pharmacist to provide the consultation, guidance, and grace needed at that moment. It is not within the vocation as Christian to recommend a different medical course of action. It is not within the vocation as pharmacist to judge or condemn a patient's choices. As a Christian pharmacist, it is within the vocation to serve the patient with all the knowledge the pharmacist has about the medication, treatments, and other potential options that may exist. It is the Christian pharmacist's vocation to help educate the patient regarding medical care so that the patient can make the decision that best reflects his or her own moral conscience. The Christian pharmacist's moral conscience can help her lead that discussion. The outcomes of these discussions and decisions can be excruciating to bear. The pharmacist's primary obligation must be to the patient in front of him in that moment. The Christian pharmacist must serve that patient as his neighbor through grace. The Christian pharmacist must remember to turn to God in times of conflict between her vocations and trust in Him to make the right choices. The Christian pharmacist can find solace in the knowledge that there are other vocations at work in these patients' lives. There are the vocations of chaplain, pastor, family, and friend who will provide guidance and God's wisdom to these individuals.

It can be particularly challenging to reconcile differences between Christian values and medical ethics or legal obligations in the profession of pharmacy. For example, what does a Christian pharmacist do when asked to dispense a medication for euthanasia or assisted suicide? How can that pharmacist reconcile his actions in the assistance of taking a life by providing the medication that causes the act to occur? According to Christianity all lives are sacred. Providing the medication that will be used to end a life seems to go directly against the commandment "You shall not murder" (Exodus 20:13). Does prescribing the medication as a pharmacist make the pharmacist a partaker in evil? Is the pharmacist guilty before God for aiding and abetting? These are questions the Christian pharmacist must take time to struggle with, reflect upon, and learn from to live out her vocation as God intends.[6]

People, including Christians, are flawed. Our flaws often appear in the dichotomy between what "could" be done and what "should" be done in healthcare. There are many potential sources of conflict between those who serve and those whom they are serving. It is good for all that God is not flawed. Martin Luther states that God uses the Christian's faith in Him for the good of others.[7] God allows people to make choices that may not align with His law, but these choices are an opportunity for God to use the Christian pharmacist to demonstrate the grace of the Gospel. The Christian pharmacist simply must have faith in God's love, mercy, and purpose for her.

Certainly, the Christian pharmacist should pray for the health and wellness of all his patients silently in his daily prayers. The Christian pharmacist could pray along with a patient if the patient asks and the pharmacist feels comfortable in that role. Yet only the Holy Spirit can

6 These cases are known in the medical ethics literature as conflicts of conscience. Many Christian pharmacists choose not to dispense medications they know will be used to end a life, just as many other Christian healthcare professionals refuse to participate in procedures they believe are inherently sinful.

7 Thesis 26 of Luther's Heidelberg Disputation states, "The law says, 'do this,' and it is never done. Grace says, 'believe in this,' and everything is already done" (*Luther's Works* 31:41).

speak to souls and bring them to Jesus. The pharmacist does not always need words to bear witness to Jesus' love.[8] As the Christian pharmacist demonstrates love to each patient as Jesus does for him, the patients will see Jesus' love as well. Then, for those patients who ask for it, the Christian pharmacist is empowered to share the love and peace that is within them through Jesus Christ.[9]

Healthcare in the United States is changing, and the pharmacy profession is changing along with it. The pharmacist's roles are expanding, and responsibilities for direct patient care are increasing. As a whole, these changes are a positive direction forward for the profession. However, with greater expectations of the professional comes greater liability on the professional who provides care. Pharmacists pursue the field of healthcare because they want to help people. They want to make a difference for the better, provide care to the suffering, aid in healing, and increase wellness in their communities. Thus, the discussion of liability due to an unintended medical error made by a pharmacist in good faith can be delicate and full of emotion. What must be remembered is that every pharmacist will make at least one error during the course of his or her professional career. Most will make many errors. This does not excuse poor choices or excuse the pharmacist for making a mistake. Rather, this knowledge provides context for the discussion of liability. As imperfect and flawed creatures, we inevitably make errors in choice. When medical errors happen within the pharmacy profession, the result could be severe harm to the patient. For a pharmacist who has taken the oath of a pharmacist, an error can be heart-wrenching, bringing on feelings of shame and guilt over the wrong course of action. When a pharmacist revisits the words, "I will apply my knowledge, experience, and skills to the best of my ability to assure optimal outcomes for my patients," after making a medical error, it can lead to the feeling that the pharmacist is a fraud in his profession. The pharmacist may feel

8 Peter's words to wives of unbelieving husbands are relevant: "Even if some do not obey the word, they may be won without a word by the conduct of their wives, when they see your respectful and pure conduct" (1 Peter 3:1–2).

9 See 1 Peter 3:15: "But in your hearts honor Christ the Lord as holy, always being prepared to make a defense to anyone who asks you for a reason for the hope that is in you; yet do it with gentleness and respect."

that he couldn't possibly be worthy of the responsibility laid upon him through his profession of pharmacist. For a Christian pharmacist who has additionally vowed to "love your neighbor as yourself" (Leviticus 19:18), this pain, shame, and guilt can be debilitating.

As a practicing pharmacist, I have made unintended medical errors. I experience painful regret, because some of these errors have caused harm to my patients, the very individuals I have pledged my life to serve. How can we, as pharmacists, carry the burden of guilt that comes from making a mistake and harming someone? How can we, as Christian pharmacists, continue to serve other patients in love and joy while we carry the shame, guilt, and feelings of unworthiness of our title of Doctor? Through Scripture and theological counsel, I have learned that I cannot remove this shadow from my soul alone. Alone, I cannot lift this burden. I need Jesus' blood of forgiveness to release me from the burden of breaking my professional oath. I need to return to the infinite refuge of Christ to receive the forgiveness He won for me on the cross. As Christian pharmacists, we can find solace in the knowledge that our mistakes are forgiven. Then, strengthened by His forgiveness, we can continue to practice our profession out of Christian love for those we serve. That same love moves us to use the experience gained and the lessons learned from failure to enhance future decision-making.

In his Table of Duties, Luther instructs everyone in all vocations by quoting Romans 13:9, "Love your neighbor as yourself." Vocation is about giving of yourself for your fellow man. It is about using your God-given gifts for others. It is difficult, if not impossible, to love others fully if we do not value the particular gifts God gave each of us as individuals, the forgiveness we have in Christ, and His call to serve others in our vocations. Only then can we have the strength to show grace joyously to those we serve. We must remember that we cannot do any of these things without the strength that God provides.[10] Primarily, we ask

10 The apostle Peter tells how we are provided with the strength to serve: "As each has received a gift, use it to serve one another, as good stewards of God's varied grace: whoever speaks, as one who speaks oracles of God; whoever serves, as one who serves by the strength that God supplies—in order that in everything God may be glorified through Jesus Christ. To Him belong glory and dominion forever and ever. Amen" (1 Peter 4:10–11).

God to give us strength, discernment, and wisdom through the Holy Spirit to allow us to emulate the love of our Teacher, Jesus, successfully and completely. This needs to be done not once, not twice, but continually along our journey through our multiple vocational paths. In the pharmacy world we talk about the half-life of drugs. The half-life is how long it takes for the drug amount in our body to reduce by half, to be half as effective or half as strong as it was when it first reached its peak point after administration. Drugs that have a short half-life do not stick around in the blood stream very long. These drugs need to be administered often to keep them at the proper level to work in the patient's body like they should. On our own, our commitment to serve the way Jesus taught us to serve has a short half-life. We continually need to seek God's wisdom in His Word and ask the Holy Spirit for His assistance to strengthen and preserve us amidst the challenges of the world and to foster in us the servant attitude we need to succeed in our vocational roles.

As you move forward with dedication to serving through your vocational masks everyone whom God created, I encourage you to read Scripture and pray. Sit quietly with the Lord and give Him your concerns. Study what He has said to you in Scripture, and follow His call. Below is a prayer that may get you started on this journey to live out your vocational calling as a Christian pharmacist.

> Dear Father in heaven,
>
> Thank You for the opportunity to be Your servant and for the guidance You give through Your Scripture. Thank You for sending Your Son, Jesus Christ, to model true service to others through love. Help us to use Your teachings as we serve those around us through the profession of pharmacy. Please send the Holy Spirit to fill our hearts and minds with Your grace and love so that we can glorify Your name through our many vocational masks. Bring discernment to our decisions, humility to our

approach, and kindness to our words. Give us wisdom in dealing with conflict, give us patience with those around us, and inspire our forgiveness to those who may do us harm. Help us to maintain our commitment of love for all people. Forgive us for Jesus' sake when we fail. Be with us as we serve and use us to bring all into Your holy kingdom.

In Jesus' name we pray. Amen.

INDEX